American Lives 3

Readings and Language Activities

Gail Feinstein Forman
Developmental Reading and English Language Instructor
San Diego City College

New Readers Press

For Mike and Mel—
a Tom Sawyer and Huckleberry Finn who warm our hearts and share our love

The author and New Readers Press have used all reasonable skill and care to ensure that the historical information presented in this book is accurate. A list of the references consulted and the notes identifying the sources of quotations appears on pages 109–112.

Cover Library of Congress, Prints and Photographs Division LC-USZ62-57849; p. 4, 18, 39, 60, 95 © 2005 www.clipart.com; p. 4 Library of Congress, Prints and Photographs Division LC-USZ62-13002; p. 11 Library of Congress, Prints and Photographs Division LC-USZ62-117117; p. 11 National Archives and Records Administration; p. 18 Library of Congress, Prints and Photographs Division LC-USZ62-20214; p. 25 Library of Congress, Prints and Photographs Division LC-USZ62-15887; p. 25 Library of Congress, Prints and Photographs Division LC-USZ62-93268; p. 32 Library of Congress, Prints & Photographs Division, Detroit Publishing Company Collection, LC-D4-3638; p. 32 Library of Congress, Prints and Photographs Division LC-USZ62-11212; p. 39 Library of Congress, Prints and Photographs Division LC-USZ62-57849; p. 46 Library of Congress, Prints and Photographs Division LC-USZ61-791; p. 46 Library of Congress, Prints and Photographs Division LC-USZ62-28195; p. 53 Library of Congress, Prints and Photographs Division LC-USZ62-75578; p. 53 Library of Congress, Prints and Photographs Division LC-USZC2-1778; p. 60 Library of Congress, Prints and Photographs Division LC-USZ62-128944; p. 67 Library of Congress, Prints & Photographs Division, FSA/OWI Collection, LC-USW3-057670-C; p. 67 Library of Congress, Prints and Photographs Division LC-USZ62-36966; p. 74 AP/Wide World Photos; p. 74 Library of Congress, Prints & Photographs Division, FSA/OWI Collection, LC-USF34-083131-C; p. 81 Picture History; p. 81 Tim Graham/Hulton Archive/Getty Images; p. 88 © Bettmann/CORBIS; p. 88 Angel Franco/Hulton Archive/Getty Images; p. 95 Northwest Indian Fisheries Commission; p. 102 Barbara Laing/Time & Life Pictures/Getty Images; p. 102 Richard Howard/Time & Life Pictures/Getty Images

American Lives: Readings and Language Activities, Book 3
ISBN 1-978-1-56420-434-9

Copyright © 2005 New Readers Press
New Readers Press
ProLiteracy's Publishing Division
104 Marcellus Street, Syracuse, New York 13204
www.newreaderspress.com

Printed in the United States of America
9 8 7 6 5 4

Proceeds from the sale of New Readers Press materials support professional development, training, and technical assistance programs of ProLiteracy that benefit local literacy programs in the U.S. and around the globe.

Acquisitions Editor: Paula L. Schlusberg
Content Editor: Judi Lauber
Design and Production Manager: Andrea Woodbury
Photo Illustrations: Brian Quoss
Illustrations: Carolyn Boehmer, Amy Simons
Production Specialist: Maryellen Casey, Jeffrey R. Smith
Cover Design: Kimbrly Koennecke

Contents

John Adams

"The Revolution was in the minds and hearts of the people."

—*John Adams*[1]

Pre-Reading Questions

1. Read the words below the title. What is a revolution? What do you think that John Adams meant by these words?

2. The American Revolution was important in U.S. history. What do you know about the Revolution? When did it begin? Why did it happen?

Reading Preview

John Adams was the second president of the United States. He is called "the voice of independence."[2] He was part of the important events that led to the birth of this country. His ideas helped shape the United States.

John Adams

John Adams always thought that reading and studying were important. When he was a child, he was an avid reader. He later became an important leader in the early United States.

Adams was born in Braintree, Massachusetts, on October 19, 1735. His father and mother encouraged him in his education. He became an independent thinker. He could write and speak clearly on complex topics. When he had to make a difficult decision, Adams turned to books. He believed that history and great writers could teach lessons for the present.

Adams practiced law in Braintree and in nearby towns. When he went to Weymouth, Massachusetts, he stayed with the Reverend Smith. There he met the minister's daughter Abigail. John and Abigail fell in love and married in 1764. During their long marriage, they were always best friends. When they were apart, they wrote long letters to each other.

When John and Abigail married, the American colonies were changing. The first British settlers had arrived in America in the early 1600s. They had depended completely on Britain. Their government was controlled by the British. They used only British goods. The colonists felt like British citizens.

By the mid-1700s, however, the colonists were developing a new cultural identity. They had their own farms, businesses, and groups. And they were becoming more diverse. Immigrants were arriving from many countries. The colonists started to think of themselves as Americans.

Then Britain wanted to pay some debts. It imposed taxes on the colonies for the first time. Many colonists, including Adams, protested. They forced Britain to repeal, or take away, most of the taxes. Britain kept only the tax on tea.

Another British law allowed soldiers to search a colonist's home at any time. Adams opposed this law publicly. He said that the colonists had liberties that were given to them by God. One liberty was the right to privacy in their homes. Adams said that even a king could not take away this right. He said that the colonists should not accept unfair laws.

Adams spoke out against the British. But he also believed that everyone should get a fair trial. So in 1770, he defended a group of British soldiers. The soldiers had fired guns into a crowd of colonists. They killed five colonists and were accused of murder. This event became known as the Boston Massacre. Adams did not like the British. But he put aside his feelings. He defended the soldiers in court according to the law.

In 1773 Britain passed the Tea Act. Under this law, the colonists could buy tea at a low price. But they still had to pay the tax. Some colonists protested this tax. In December 1773, they went on board British ships and threw tea into Boston Harbor. For punishment, Britain closed the harbor in 1774.

Adams and other colonists were angry. Of the 13 colonies, 12 sent delegates to a meeting in Philadelphia. Adams represented Massachusetts. The delegates talked about how to defend their rights. They agreed to boycott British goods. They demanded that Britain repeal the tax on tea. And they talked about becoming a separate country.

On April 19, 1775, British soldiers were marching to Concord, Massachusetts. The colonists had weapons there, and the soldiers planned to destroy them. Colonial soldiers met the British at Lexington. This battle began the American Revolution. Colonial delegates soon met again in Philadelphia. Not all the colonies wanted independence. Adams gave a two-hour speech. He spoke with great emotion about the need for independence. Later, Thomas Jefferson wrote that Adams spoke "with a power of thought and expression that moved us from our seats."[3] Adams's speech persuaded many delegates to vote for independence.

In 1782, the Congress chose Adams to go to Paris. There, he, Benjamin Franklin, and John Jay negotiated a treaty—a formal agreement—with Britain. This treaty ended the war. Britain recognized the United States as an independent country.

John Adams continued to serve his country in later years. He was the first vice president of the United States from 1789 to 1796. And he was president from 1797 to 1800. In 1801 he returned to Massachusetts. For the next 25 years, he wrote about his life. He also exchanged letters with family and friends.

Adams died on July 4, 1826—the 50th anniversary of the Declaration of Independence. He was 90 years old. One of the last things that Adams said was, "Thomas Jefferson survives."[4] He did not know that Jefferson had died just a few hours before.

Comprehension

Check the correct answer.

1. John Adams believed that

   _____ a. education was not important.

   _____ b. books had many lessons to teach.

   _____ c. learning about the past doesn't help the present.

2. When Adams married Abigail Smith in 1764,

   _____ a. colonists still felt like British citizens.

   _____ b. Americans were developing their own cultural identity.

   _____ c. colonists depended on the British for their needs.

3. Even though Adams opposed British rule,

   _____ a. he agreed to defend British soldiers in court.

   _____ b. he wanted colonists to buy only British goods.

   _____ c. he never spoke out publicly against Britain.

4. Adams said that the colonists

   _____ a. should not protest against Britain.

   _____ b. should reject unfair British laws.

   _____ c. should remain British citizens.

5. To persuade delegates that they should vote for independence,

   _____ a. Adams made an emotional two-hour speech.

   _____ b. Adams asked Jefferson to make a speech.

   _____ c. Adams wrote the Declaration of Independence.

6. After the Revolution, Adams continued to serve his country

   _____ a. as the U.S. ambassador to France.

   _____ b. as vice president and then as president.

   _____ c. as Secretary of State.

7. July 4, 1826, was an important day in U.S. history because

   _____ a. colonists hung flags from their homes.

   _____ b. Adams and Thomas Jefferson both died that day.

   _____ c. the Declaration of Independence was signed.

Sequence

Work with a partner. Number the events in the correct order.

_____ Adams marries Abigail Smith.

_____ The American Revolution ends.

_____ Colonists throw tea into Boston Harbor.

_____ Adams becomes a lawyer.

_____ John Adams and Thomas Jefferson die.

_____ Adams becomes vice president of the United States.

Vocabulary

Look at these words from the reading. Put a check next to words that you know. Underline words that you don't know yet. Find the words in the reading. Try to guess their meanings.

accused	cultural identity	diverse	negotiate
avid	debts	imposed	persuaded

Use the words to fill in the blanks in the story.

When John Adams was young, he was an _____ reader. When he grew
                                              1

up, he became a lawyer and then married Abigail Smith. During the early

years of their marriage, America was developing a new _____. The
                                                                2

colonists were more and more _____, and they began to feel American,
                                       3

not British. So when Britain _____ taxes on the colonies to pay
                                      4

_____, the colonists protested. Adams opposed the British. Even so, he
        5

defended British soldiers who were _____ of murdering five colonists.
                                            6

Then in 1775, the American Revolution began. Adams made an emotional

speech at a meeting of colonial delegates. His speech _____ many
                                                                7

delegates to vote for independence. At the end of the Revolution, Adams

helped _____ the peace treaty between the United States and Britain.
            8

Reading a Time Line

A time line shows dates and events in order on a line.

Important Events in Early American History

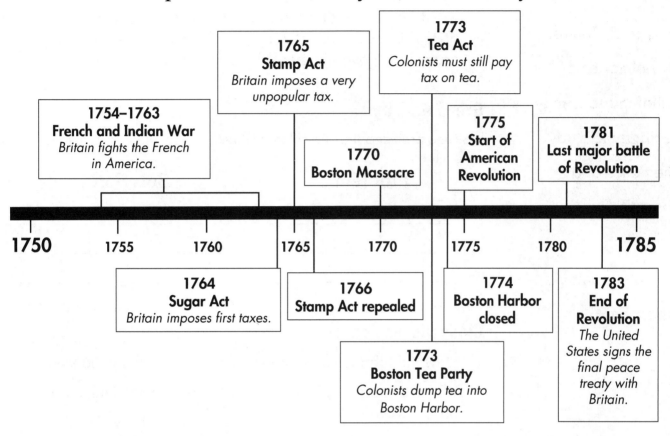

Answer the questions. Use information from the time line.

1. From 1754 to 1763, Britain fought the _____ War.

2. Britain passed and then repealed the _____ Act.

3. The Boston Massacre happened in _____.

4. The American Revolution lasted _____ years.

5. List three important events that happened after the Boston Massacre but before the start of the American Revolution.

   a. _____

   b. _____

   c. _____

Discuss: Look at the events that you listed in item 5 above. How did these events help lead to the American Revolution?

Adams said, "I must study politics and war that my sons may have liberty to study mathematics and philosophy."[6]

What do you think that he meant?

Connecting Today and Yesterday

1. How do Americans express political opinions today? How did the early colonists express political opinions? How are these ways alike? How are they different?

2. What does the right to free speech mean in the United States? Does it mean that a person can always speak openly against the government? Why or why not?

Group Activity

List three problems that the colonists faced. Then write their solution for each one.

Problem	Solution
1. _____	1. _____
2. _____	2. _____
3. _____	3. _____

Class Discussion

1. How did John Adams's personality make him a good leader?

2. Why did Adams agree to defend the British soldiers in the Boston Massacre?

3. Adams's speech persuaded delegates to vote for independence. What do you think that he said?

4. Look at your problem-solution list from the Group Activity above. How did the problems and solutions help lead to American independence? If you were a colonist, would you have voted for independence? Explain.

5. Why did Adams say "Thomas Jefferson survives" when he was dying himself?

Reflections

1. What was the most interesting thing that you read in this lesson?

2. Can you use anything from John Adams's story in your own life? Explain.

3. How can you learn more about John Adams or the American Revolution?

Thomas Jefferson

*"The God who gave us life gave
us liberty at the same time."*

—*Thomas Jefferson*[1]

Pre-Reading Questions

1. Read the words below the title. What do you think that they
   mean? Do you agree or disagree with this idea? Explain.

2. What do you know about Thomas Jefferson? Why was
   freedom important to him?

Reading Preview

Thomas Jefferson was important during the Revolution and
the years that followed. He wrote beautifully about freedom
and equality. His words helped shape the American belief
in human rights.

Thomas Jefferson

Thomas Jefferson spent almost 40 years in public service. But his favorite activity was returning to his land. Jefferson loved to ride horses and explore his property. He felt closely connected to his land.

Jefferson was born on a plantation, or large farm, in Shadwell, Virginia, in 1743. His parents were wealthy tobacco farmers. Jefferson had a curious mind. He was interested in everything around him. He read books on many subjects, including science. He did many experiments on his farm. At college, he was a disciplined student. Each day, he studied for 15 hours and practiced the violin for 3 hours. That left only 6 hours to eat and sleep. After college, he studied law. He became well-known for his sharp legal mind.

Jefferson was an avid reader. The new philosophy of the Enlightenment influenced him. Enlightenment philosophers said that each person has natural rights. Jefferson believed that people have the right to create their own destiny. He believed that kings, government, and religion should not control people. Jefferson also thought that a central government should have limited power. He did not want government to interfere with people's private lives. This was a radical idea. In Jefferson's time, most people lived under a king or a dictator.

Jefferson entered government service in 1769. He became a representative in the Virginia legislature. Jefferson was never a good public speaker. But, in John Adams's words, Jefferson had "a masterly pen."[2] In 1774, he wrote *A Summary View of the Rights of British America.* This document said that the colonies had the right to govern themselves. It said that they should be able to live without British control. Jefferson's writing and belief in individual rights impressed the Second Continental Congress. The Congress asked him to write the Declaration of Independence.

Jefferson was Secretary of State under President George Washington from 1790 to 1793. He often disagreed with Alexander Hamilton, the Secretary of the Treasury. Because of their conflict, two political parties developed. Jefferson led the Republican Party. The Republicans opposed a strong central government. They wanted good relations with France instead of Britain. And they wanted to keep the U.S. economy based on farming. Hamilton led the Federalist Party. The Federalists wanted a strong central government. They wanted close ties with England instead of France. And they wanted an economy based on manufacturing.

In 1797, Jefferson became vice president. President John Adams was a Federalist. The Federalists feared war with France. In 1798, Adams supported the Alien and Sedition Acts. These laws said that the federal government could expel foreigners during a war if the president believed that they were dangerous to the United States. They also made it illegal to speak against the president or Congress. Jefferson opposed these laws. He believed that they were unfair to people from France. He also believed that they prevented free speech.

In 1800, Jefferson ran against John Adams for president. The campaign was bitter. There was violence between members of the two parties. Some people feared a civil war. The election resulted in a tie vote in the Electoral College. So the vote went to the House of Representatives. Finally, Jefferson won. It was a peaceful transfer of political power—the first in the United States, and one of the first in the world.

Jefferson was president for two terms, until 1808. While he was president, the United States bought the Louisiana Territory from France. This area stretched from the Mississippi River to the Rocky Mountains. The new territory doubled the size of the United States. Jefferson enjoyed his job in his first term. During his second term, however, his daughter Martha died in childbirth. His wife, Martha, had also died in childbirth years earlier. After his daughter's death, Jefferson lost some of his interest in politics.

After he was president, Jefferson continued building Monticello, a large home that he had designed. He also designed buildings for the University of Virginia.

Many people are surprised by a major contradiction in Jefferson's life. The man who wrote "All men are created equal" was also a slave owner. Jefferson wrote that he hated slavery. He believed that slaves would be freed in the next generation. But he himself did not work to end slavery. Jefferson tried to treat his slaves well. He may have had children with one of his slaves. However, when he died, he left instructions to free only some of his slaves, not all of them.

Jefferson wanted people to remember him for writing the Declaration of Independence. He died on July 4, 1826. It was the 50th anniversary of the day that the Declaration was signed.

"I have sworn upon the altar of God eternal hostility against every form of tyranny over the mind of man."

—Thomas Jefferson[3]

Comprehension

Complete the sentences. Use information from the reading.

1. In college, Jefferson _____

   _____.

2. The Enlightenment philosophers believed that _____

   _____.

3. *A Summary View of the Rights of British America* said that _____

   _____.

4. The Second Continental Congress asked Jefferson to write the

   Declaration of Independence because _____

   _____.

5. Jefferson's Republican Party wanted the United States to _____

   _____.

6. The Alien and Sedition Acts allowed the government to _____

   _____.

7. The purchase of the Louisiana Territory was important because _____

   _____.

8. The main contradiction in Jefferson's life was that _____

   _____

   _____.

Summary

Check the best summary of the ideas in the reading.

_____ 1. Thomas Jefferson was a great thinker and writer. His words and leadership greatly influenced the development of the United States.

_____ 2. Thomas Jefferson had contradictions in his life. He helped start the U.S. two-party system.

Vocabulary

Look at these words from the reading. Put a check next to words that you know. Underline words that you don't know yet. Find the words in the reading. Try to guess their meanings.

campaign	destiny	expel	oppose
contradiction	disciplined	experiment	radical

Check the correct meaning for each word.

1. experiment
   - _____ a. test
   - _____ b. meeting
   - _____ c. discussion

2. disciplined
   - _____ a. self-controlled
   - _____ b. strict
   - _____ c. busy

3. destiny
   - _____ a. faraway place
   - _____ b. future life
   - _____ c. behavior

4. radical
   - _____ a. common
   - _____ b. beautiful
   - _____ c. extreme

5. expel
   - _____ a. to unite
   - _____ b. to throw out
   - _____ c. to kill

6. oppose
   - _____ a. to support
   - _____ b. to disagree with
   - _____ c. to have no opinion about

7. campaign
   - _____ a. vote
   - _____ b. political race
   - _____ c. discussion

8. contradiction
   - _____ a. something that is expected
   - _____ b. something that is unexpected
   - _____ c. something that limits free speech

Reading a Map

Physical maps show features of the land and water. **Political maps** show borders between countries, states, or other political territories. **Historical maps** show features from the past. Some maps, like this one, combine all three types. It shows physical features and political territories in North America during the early 19th century. To read this map, you need to understand the words for directions: *north, south, east,* and *west.* These directions appear on maps in a compass rose (right).

The United States in 1803

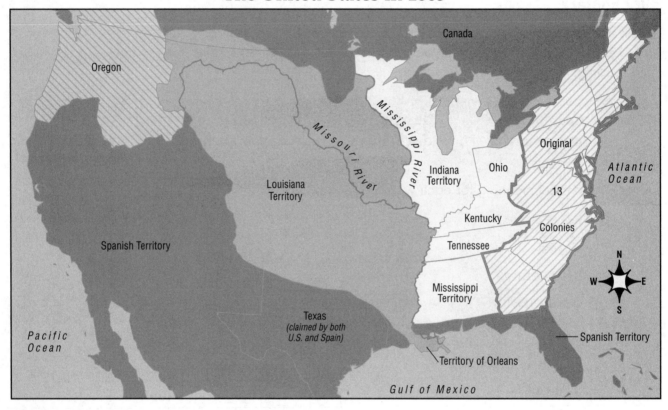

Fill in the blanks. Use information from the map. Item 1 is done for you.
Use words for directions in items 2–5.

1. Texas is _____ *south* _____ of the Louisiana Territory.

2. The larger piece of Spanish territory was _____ of the Louisiana Territory.

3. The Missouri River flows _____ toward the Indiana Territory.

4. Oregon was _____ of the larger piece of Spanish territory.

5. The territory of Orleans was _____ of the Mississippi Territory.

6. Texas was claimed by both _____ and _____.

Connecting Today and Yesterday

1. The U.S. government passed the Alien and Sedition Acts to provide security. The government wanted to expel foreigners who might be dangerous to the country. Do you think that this kind of law is fair? Why or why not?

2. Do you think that there is discrimination against any group in the United States today? Explain.

Group Activities

1. Research the qualifications for the U.S. president. What document states these qualifications? Can an immigrant be president? Can a woman be president? Why or why not?

2. Find out how the president is elected in the United States. What is the difference between popular vote and electoral vote? Why were President Adams and Vice President Jefferson from different parties? Could that happen today?

Class Discussion

1. Why is Jefferson sometimes called "the philosopher president"?

2. In Jefferson's first speech as president, he said, "We are all Republicans. We are all Federalists."[4] What did he mean? Why did he say this?

3. Why was the Louisiana Territory important to the future of the United States?

4. How can we explain Jefferson's belief in individual rights when he also owned slaves? Is it fair to judge Jefferson by today's human rights principles?

Reflections

1. What was the most interesting thing that you read in this lesson?

2. Can you use anything from Thomas Jefferson's story in your own life? Explain.

3. How can you learn more about Thomas Jefferson or the early development of the United States?

Two great heroes of the American Revolution, Adams and Jefferson, died on the same day, exactly 50 years after the Declaration of Independence was signed. Many people think that this is a strange coincidence.

What do you think?

Meriwether Lewis

*"The longest journey begins
with a single step."*

—*well-known saying*

Pre-Reading Questions

1. Read the words below the title. What do you think that they
   mean? Did you ever take a difficult journey? If so, why?

2. If you wanted to travel across North America in 1804, what
   supplies would you take? What skills would be important?

Reading Preview

In 1804, Meriwether Lewis, with William Clark, led an expedition
called the Corps of Discovery. They made a dangerous journey
across the new Louisiana Territory. They traveled from the
Missouri River to the Pacific Ocean and back again. That territory
was important for the future of the United States.

Meriwether Lewis

Meriwether Lewis was born on August 18, 1774, on a farm in Virginia. Lewis's mother was an herbalist. She took young Lewis along to explore local woods and forests. She collected herbs to use as medicine.

Lewis loved to ride horses, hike, and hunt in the forests. He felt restless on the farm. He joined the military to find adventure and contribute to history. Then, in 1801, President Thomas Jefferson needed a trustworthy personal aide. Jefferson knew the Lewis family well. So he asked Lewis to take the job. Lewis was Jefferson's aide for two years.

At the time, many people believed that there was a direct water route to Asia across northern North America. They called this route the Northwest Passage. People believed that it went west across the territory between the Missouri River and the Pacific Ocean. Maps labeled this area "unknown." People thought that it was dangerous. They believed that it had volcanoes and large, man-eating wild creatures. But Jefferson wanted to find a route across the new Louisiana Territory. He knew that this route could increase U.S. commerce.

Jefferson wanted an expedition to explore this territory. He asked Lewis to lead the expedition. Jefferson knew that Lewis was a skilled and adventurous frontiersman. He also knew that he could trust Lewis. To prepare for the journey, Jefferson sent Lewis to study science. He wanted the explorers to record their locations by the stars and land. He also wanted them to collect samples of all new plants and animals.

Jefferson also asked the expedition to build friendships with Native Americans in the new territory. He wanted to learn about their cultures. And he wanted the Native Americans to understand that he was their new leader.

Lewis asked William Clark to help lead the expedition. Lewis had served under Clark in the army. He knew that Clark was an excellent mapmaker and a courageous explorer. The expedition was called "the Corps of Discovery." The 33 members were a multi-ethnic group. Most were in the U.S. military. Clark's black slave, York, was also a member. So were a Native American woman named Sacagawea, her French Canadian husband, and their baby son. Sacagawea spoke two Native American languages. She helped translate for the expedition. Lewis also took his dog, Seaman.

This large group carried guns, ammunition, clothing, gifts for Native Americans, and other supplies. They also took scientific instruments, medicine, and books. They fit all this and themselves into a special boat and some small canoes.

The journey began on May 14, 1804. The explorers faced many problems. They survived in freezing weather. They crossed high, icy mountains where they almost died. They often did not have enough food, and they lived in cramped conditions. Several people, including Lewis, had malaria, a deadly disease that is carried by mosquitoes. Fortunately, the group got along well with the Native Americans that they encountered. Only one meeting involved violence.

Some members of the group kept journals on the trip. They reported that Lewis was a skilled commander. But they also said that he was hot-tempered and sometimes depressed. Lewis did not always seem comfortable as leader. Even so, he created a close group that worked well. The members depended on each other for emotional and spiritual support.

In November 1805, the explorers reached the Pacific Ocean. And almost a year later, on September 23, 1806, they returned to St. Louis. They had traveled 3,700 miles, mostly on foot. They learned that there was no water route from the Missouri River to the Pacific Ocean. But they mapped a land route from east to west. Now others could follow their map. The expedition also opened new trade relationships with the French and the Native Americans in the territory. It found many new animals and plants. And it brought back information about the culture and activities of 52 Native American tribes.

The U.S. government gave land and money to all the explorers except York and Sacagawea. And Jefferson appointed Lewis governor of the Louisiana Territory. However, Lewis had problems with his health. He still suffered from malaria and depression. He had many debts. And he was not an effective governor. In July 1809, he died of a gunshot wound at age 35. Most people believe that he committed suicide.

Lewis, Clark, and the Corps of Discovery probably made the most famous journey in U.S. history. This journey was a search for knowledge and a service to the country. By leading the Corps of Discovery, Lewis greatly helped the development of the new United States.

Comprehension

Check the correct answer.

1. Lewis learned about using herbs for medicine

    _____ a. from the Corps of Discovery.

    _____ b. from William Clark.

    _____ c. from his mother.

2. Jefferson asked Lewis to lead the expedition because

    _____ a. Lewis was a skilled frontiersman.

    _____ b. Lewis could make good maps.

    _____ c. Lewis had met many Native Americans.

3. People in the United States knew little about the territory west of the Missouri River, so

    _____ a. the Corps of Discovery refused to go there.

    _____ b. Jefferson didn't expect accurate maps.

    _____ c. they believed that dangerous animals lived there.

4. The 33 members of the Corps of Discovery

    _____ a. were all Native Americans.

    _____ b. were a multi-ethnic group.

    _____ c. were all military men.

5. Members of the expedition

    _____ a. had an easy trip across the continent.

    _____ b. never became ill.

    _____ c. had to live in difficult conditions.

6. As a leader, Lewis

    _____ a. always seemed at ease.

    _____ b. helped the group work well.

    _____ c. could not create a close group.

7. After the expedition returned, Lewis

    _____ a. became governor of the Louisiana Territory.

    _____ b. got married and had two children.

    _____ c. returned to military life.

Sequence

Work with a partner. Number the events in the correct order.

_____ Lewis works as President Jefferson's aide.

_____ Lewis and Clark begin their journey.

_____ Lewis learns about using herbs for medicine.

_____ Members of the Corps of Discovery receive land and money.

_____ Lewis joins the army.

_____ Sacagawea translates for the Corps of Discovery.

Vocabulary

Look at these words from the reading. Put a check next to words that you know. Underline words that you don't know yet. Find the words in the reading. Try to guess their meanings.

appointed	encountered	frontiersman	restless
cramped	expedition	herbalist	trustworthy

Use the words to fill in the blanks in the story.

When Lewis was young, he often helped his mother, who was an _____ 1

He loved the outdoors and became a skilled _____. He wanted 2

adventure and felt _____ on his family's farm, so he joined the army. 3

Then he worked as President Jefferson's aide. Jefferson asked

Lewis to lead an _____ across the Louisiana Territory. Jefferson knew 4

that Lewis would be a _____ leader. Lewis and the Corps of Discovery 5

_____ many Native American tribes and mapped a route to the Pacific 6

Ocean. They also faced many dangers. They often had little food.

They suffered from illness and _____ living conditions. After the 7

expedition returned, Lewis was _____ governor of the Louisiana 8

Territory. He died of a gunshot wound in 1809.

Reading a Map

Physical maps show features of land and water. **Political maps** show borders between countries, states, or other organized territories. **Historical maps** show features from the past. Some maps, like this one, combine all three types. It shows the route of Lewis and Clark and the places and physical features in the region that they explored. For comparison, it also shows the borders of modern-day states.

Route of the Lewis and Clark Expedition

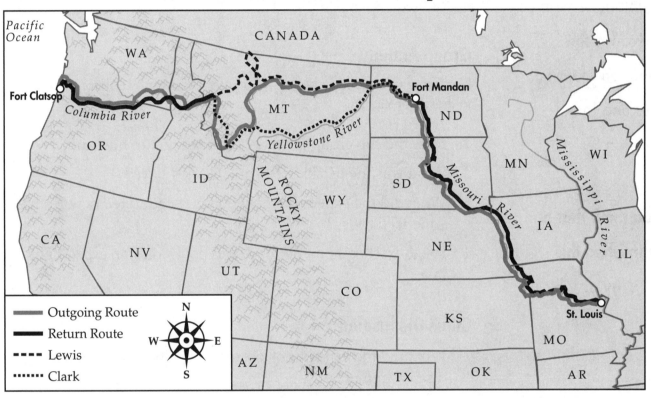

Answer the questions. Use information from the map.

1. At the start of the trip, what river did the expedition travel north on?

   _____

2. What is the name of the farthest point west that the expedition reached?
   What state is it in? _____

3. On what major river did the expedition travel in Washington state?

   _____

4. Clark and Lewis took two different routes back. On what river did Clark
   travel without Lewis? _____

5. Where did the expedition complete its trip? _____

On his 31st birthday, Lewis wrote in his journal that he wanted "to advance the information of the succeeding [next] generation."[2]

Do you think that he accomplished this goal? Why or why not?

Connecting Today and Yesterday

1. The Corps of Discovery did not have accurate information about the territory that it was exploring. How were early space flights like the expedition?

2. Jefferson wanted to learn about the culture of Native Americans in the Louisiana Territory. But he also wanted the Native Americans to accept him as their leader. How did his attitude reflect the future of Native Americans in the United States?

Group Activity

Find more information about the Corps of Discovery. Look for answers to these questions.

1. How did the group meet Sacagawea and her husband?

2. What was the trip like for York, Clark's slave?

3. What did the expedition do when it encountered new Native American tribes?

4. What exact equipment, food, and books did the expedition take?

Class Discussion

1. What did the expedition accomplish? What was its main disappointment?

2. Why didn't York or Sacagawea receive land or money?

3. Why were William Clark's mapmaking skills important?

4. Describe Lewis's personality. Do you think that he was a good choice to lead the expedition? Why or why not?

Reflections

1. What was the most interesting thing that you read in this lesson?

2. Can you use anything from Meriwether Lewis's story in your own life? Explain.

3. How can you learn more about Meriwether Lewis or the Corps of Discovery?

Frederick Douglass

"You have seen how a man was made a slave; you shall see how a slave was made a man."

—*Frederick Douglass*[1]

Pre-Reading Questions

1. Read the words below the title. What do you think that they mean?

2. Did you ever hear of the Underground Railroad? What was it, and when was it used? Where was it used?

Reading Preview

Frederick Douglass was a slave who escaped to freedom. He became famous for his antislavery speeches. He also wrote a widely read book about his life as a slave. Douglass was the first black citizen to hold a high position in the U.S. government. He became an adviser to President Lincoln on black civil rights.

Frederick Douglass

The black abolitionist Frederick Douglass had the name Frederick Bailey at birth. He was born into slavery on Holmes Hill Farm in Maryland in 1817.

Slavery was very profitable for plantation owners in the South. Plantations were large farms. Cotton had become the main farm crop. The plantations sold cotton to the northern states and to Britain. Northern and British factories made it into textiles. Cotton was an $8 billion business. For plantation owners, it was cheaper to buy slaves than to pay laborers. By 1830, there were more than two million slaves in the United States.

Slaves were considered property. People often did not treat them as human beings. Slave children ate food from pails for feeding pigs. Frequently they had no beds or blankets.

Bailey worked on Thomas Auld's plantation and hated the terrible conditions. Fortunately, Auld's wife liked Bailey's quiet manner. When he was a teenager, she sent him to Baltimore. There, he worked for her brother-in-law, Hugh Auld.

In Baltimore, Bailey took care of Hugh Auld's infant son and went on errands. Auld's wife read aloud to Bailey from the Bible and started to teach him to read and write. But her husband found out, and he refused to let her teach Bailey anymore. He said that slaves had to be illiterate or they would learn to think and act independently.

Bailey knew that reading could teach him many things and wanted to continue his lessons. He secretly got poor white children to teach him. He paid them with pieces of bread.

When Hugh Auld died, Bailey was forced to return to Thomas Auld's plantation. He had a harsh life there as a field worker. Bailey organized religious services for the slaves. When Auld found out, he beat Bailey repeatedly.

Later, Bailey planned to escape with others on the farm, but the plot was discovered. All the men, including Bailey, went to prison. Thomas Auld went to the prison and bought Bailey back. He then sent Bailey to work for a local shipbuilder. Bailey learned how to caulk, or seal, ship seams. He earned a good salary, but he had to give most of the money to Auld. During that time, Bailey attended the East Baltimore Mental Improvement Society.

This was a group of educated free blacks. He learned public-speaking skills, and he met his wife, Anna Murray. Bailey didn't want to be a slave, and he decided to escape.

Bailey disguised himself as a sailor and got some false papers. He took a train to Philadelphia and then to New York City. In New York, Bailey lived with David Ruggles. Ruggles's home was a stop on the Underground Railroad. Bailey and his wife then moved to New Bedford, Massachusetts. Again, he worked as a caulker. Bailey was afraid that Auld would send slave catchers after him, so he changed his name to Douglass.

In 1841, Douglass spoke at an Anti-Slavery Society meeting. The famous abolitionist William Lloyd Garrison, editor of *The Liberator,* heard him. Garrison was impressed with Douglass's eloquent speech. He hired Douglass to travel around the country and describe the terrible conditions of slaves.

Douglass decided also to write the story of his life. The book was called *A Narrative of the Life of Frederick Douglass, An American Slave.* It was published in May 1845.

Douglass was still afraid of being caught as a slave. He moved to England, where slavery was illegal. He spoke throughout England and Ireland, building support for the abolitionist movement. After two years, two English friends gave Douglass the money to buy his freedom—$710.96. On December 5, 1846, Douglass became a free man.

Douglass returned to the United States. He moved to Rochester, New York, and started the nation's best-known black newspaper, *The North Star.* In his articles, Douglass supported black civil rights and voting rights for blacks and women. Douglass's Rochester home became a stop on the Underground Railroad. He helped hundreds of slaves on their way to freedom.

In 1863, during the Civil War, black men could join the northern army. But they received less pay than whites and had inferior living conditions. Douglass was upset. He discussed these issues at a meeting with President Lincoln. At a second meeting in 1864, Lincoln asked Douglass to create an evacuation plan for slaves in case the North lost the war.

Douglass moved to Washington, D.C., in 1872. The plantation where he had been a slave was nearby, and he decided to visit it. Thomas Auld, the owner, was now old and weak. Auld and

"A new world had opened upon me."

—*Frederick Douglass*[2]

Douglass talked for two hours. Auld said that slavery was necessary, but he apologized to Douglass for his bad treatment.

In 1895, Douglass died of a heart attack. Black public schools closed for a day. Many black families traveled to Rochester to honor this great man. His support for black civil rights shaped the history of black Americans.

Comprehension

Complete the sentences. Use information from the reading.

1. Bailey knew a lot about slavery because _____

   _____.

2. When Hugh Auld found out that his wife was teaching Bailey

   to read and write, he _____

   _____.

3. After Thomas Auld bought Bailey back from prison, Bailey _____

   _____.

4. To escape to New York, Bailey _____

   _____.

5. Bailey changed his name to Douglass because _____

   _____.

6. After William Lloyd Garrison heard Douglass speak against

   slavery, _____

   _____.

7. Douglass moved to England because _____

   _____.

8. Douglass spoke to Abraham Lincoln about _____

   _____.

Sequence

Work with a partner. Number the events in the correct order.

_____ Douglass writes *A Narrative of the Life of Frederick Douglass.*

_____ Douglass meets Abraham Lincoln.

_____ Douglass buys his freedom.

_____ Douglass starts *The North Star.*

_____ William Lloyd Garrison hires Douglass to speak about slavery.

Vocabulary

Look at these words from the reading. Put a check next to words that you know. Underline words that you don't know yet. Find the words in the reading. Try to guess their meanings.

| caulk | eloquent | illiterate | plot |
| disguise | evacuation | inferior | textiles |

Check the correct meaning for each word.

1. textiles

   _____ a. cloth

   _____ b. guns

   _____ c. hats

2. illiterate

   _____ a. not able to read

   _____ b. able to read only the Bible

   _____ c. not interested in reading

3. plot

   _____ a. story

   _____ b. plan

   _____ c. price

4. caulk

   _____ a. to cook for sailors

   _____ b. to draw on a blackboard

   _____ c. to fill cracks to keep out water

5. disguise

   _____ a. to be unhappy

   _____ b. to change appearance

   _____ c. to work hard

6. eloquent

   _____ a. long and boring

   _____ b. clear and powerful

   _____ c. needing a translator

7. inferior

   _____ a. colder

   _____ b. worse in quality

   _____ c. fancier

8. evacuation

   _____ a. removing trash

   _____ b. planning for a new city

   _____ c. escaping from danger

Reading a Map

Physical maps show features of land and water. **Political maps** show borders between countries, states, or other organized territories. **Historical maps** show features from the past. Some maps, like this one, combine all three types. It shows physical and political features of the United States in the mid-19th century. It also shows the major routes of the Underground Railroad.

Major Routes of the Underground Railroad

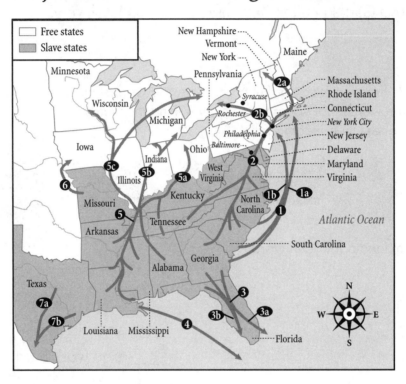

Answer the questions. Use information from the map.

1. What slave states did the Underground Railroad go through? _____

   _____

2. Which route from south to north looks the longest? _____

3. What waterway did slaves use to go from South Carolina to

   New York City? _____

4. Re-read the information about the escape route that Frederick

   Douglass used. Which route on the map matches his? _____

5. Which route would bring escaping slaves to Douglass's home

   in Rochester, New York? _____

Connecting Today and Yesterday

1. Slavery became illegal in the United States in 1865. Does slavery still exist in the world? Where? What kind of slavery exists there?

2. Many African Americans had ancestors who were slaves. Do you think that this fact influences black Americans today? Explain.

Group Activities

1. When Douglass visited Thomas Auld, they talked for two hours. What do you think that they said? Create a dialogue and role-play it.

2. Research the ship *Amistad.* Learn about the African slaves on the ship and how they fought to gain their freedom.

Class Discussion

1. What events in Douglass's life show inner strength and courage?

2. Why was reading important to Douglass?

3. Why did William Lloyd Garrison want Douglass to speak about his life as a slave?

4. How did Douglass support civil rights for black people and voting rights for women?

5. Some people think that the U.S. government should pay money to descendants of slaves. What do you think?

Reflections

1. What was the most interesting thing that you read in this lesson?

2. Can you use anything from Frederick Douglass's story in your own life? Explain.

3. How can you learn more about Frederick Douglass or slavery in the United States?

John F. Kennedy wrote, "A man does what he must . . . in spite of obstacles and dangers."[3]

How is this statement true about Frederick Douglass?

Harriet Beecher Stowe

Uncle Tom's Cabin *was "the greatest work of its kind which has appeared in half a century."*

—*book review in the* Providence Mirror, *1852*[1]

Pre-Reading Questions

1. Read the words below the title. What do you think makes a great book?

2. Harriet Beecher Stowe wanted to end slavery in the United States. But many people—even people who did not own slaves—wanted to keep slavery. Why did people disagree about slavery?

Reading Preview

Harriet Beecher Stowe wrote *Uncle Tom's Cabin.* It showed many readers the terrible conditions of slavery. *Uncle Tom's Cabin* has become one of the world's most famous books. It has been translated into at least 58 languages.

Harriet Beecher Stowe

Harriet Beecher Stowe grew up in a world of progressive ideas. She was born in Litchfield, Connecticut, in 1811. Her father, Lyman Beecher, was a preacher. He was strict with his children. Her mother was well educated. She tutored her children in French. She taught them English and French literature while they did household chores together. Sadly, her mother died when Harriet was five years old. At age 13, Harriet went to Hartford, Connecticut, to live at her sister Catherine's school. At this school, she began to develop her writing skill. She was later a teacher there.

In 1832, the Beecher family, including Harriet, moved to Cincinnati, Ohio. Lyman Beecher led a social and writing club in his home. Harriet attended the club's weekly discussions. Club members talked about important social issues of the day, particularly slavery. One member was Calvin Stowe, a minister and teacher. Harriet Beecher and Calvin Stowe married in 1836.

The Stowes and the Beechers were abolitionists. Many abolitionists believed that, according to the Bible, it was wrong to own slaves. They wanted to abolish, or stop, the entire system of buying and selling slaves. Sometimes there was violence between abolitionists and people who wanted to keep slavery. Once, Edward Beecher, Harriet's brother, was almost killed for his beliefs. He was visiting his friend, Elijah Lovejoy, the editor of an antislavery newspaper. That day, an angry crowd killed Lovejoy because of his opinions.

The Stowes had seven children. In 1849, their 18-month-old son, Charley, died of cholera. His death filled Harriet with terrible grief. In May 1850, Calvin Stowe became a professor at Bowdoin College, so the family moved to Maine. Calvin hoped that the move would help heal Harriet's pain. In Maine, she started writing about social issues. She poured out her emotions in her writings.

Harriet Beecher Stowe wrote short stories for a magazine called *The National Era.* These stories included one about the Fugitive Slave Act. Under this law, anyone who fed or helped a runaway slave would be punished. On the other hand, people who returned slaves to their masters would be paid for their services. This law made Stowe angry, and she wanted to show its effects. She wrote a story about fugitive slaves who could not get food or shelter.

The editor of *The National Era* encouraged Stowe to write a book about slavery. Many people did not know how slaves lived in the South. He thought that she could introduce more people to the terrible inhumanity of slavery. Stowe was busy with her children and her household, but she made time for this book too. She hoped that it would help the United States abolish slavery.

She called her book *Uncle Tom's Cabin.* She wrote in a personal style and spoke to the reader directly. She showed that slaves were human beings with needs and wants like everyone else. The main black character in her book was a slave, Uncle Tom. Tom fights against his masters. He refuses to tell where runaway slaves are hiding. This action leads to his own cruel death.

Stowe wrote about the main white family in the book with some sympathy. However, she showed that the white slave trader, Simon Legree, was a terrible person. Legree only wanted to profit from buying and selling slaves. He would do anything to make money.

Uncle Tom's Cabin was told from the heart. It became the best-selling book of its time. It sold more than 300,000 copies. Stowe earned more than $10,000 in three months. This was more money than most people made in a lifetime.

Uncle Tom's Cabin also affected the Civil War. After reading *Uncle Tom's Cabin,* many men joined the army of the North. They wanted to fight against slavery. Many soldiers carried two books with them into battle—the Bible and *Uncle Tom's Cabin.*

In 1862, Stowe met President Lincoln at the White House. Lincoln admired *Uncle Tom's Cabin.* There is a legend that he said jokingly, "So you're the little woman who wrote the book that started this Great War!"[2]

Uncle Tom's Cabin became famous all over the world. Stowe traveled in the United States and Europe to talk about her book and her ideas. After the Civil War, she continued to write. Her books supported more freedom for blacks. She also advocated voting rights for women. She died in 1896, two weeks before her 85th birthday.

Comprehension

Check the correct answer.

1. Harriet Beecher Stowe was raised in a family that

   _____ a. had little education.

   _____ b. encouraged reading, writing, and thinking.

   _____ c. thought that women didn't need an education.

2. Harriet Beecher met her husband, Calvin Stowe,

   _____ a. when she visited her sister's school.

   _____ b. at a club that met in her father's house.

   _____ c. while she was teaching.

3. Calvin Stowe hoped that moving to Maine

   _____ a. would increase the family's income.

   _____ b. would give Harriet a large garden to enjoy.

   _____ c. would help Harriet get over the death of their son.

4. When Stowe learned about the Fugitive Slave Act,

   _____ a. she was angry.

   _____ b. she thought that it was a fair law.

   _____ c. she felt encouraged.

5. When Stowe wrote *Uncle Tom's Cabin,* she

   _____ a. moved out of her home and focused on writing.

   _____ b. still ran the household while she was writing.

   _____ c. paid no attention to her children.

6. *Uncle Tom's Cabin*

   _____ a. describes only the lives of slaves.

   _____ b. describes the lives of slaves and slave owners.

   _____ c. presents a slave trader as a hero.

7. *Uncle Tom's Cabin* was so moving that

   _____ a. many northern soldiers carried it into battle.

   _____ b. Stowe traveled to Asia to talk about it.

   _____ c. every American bought a copy of it.

Sequence

Work with a partner. Number the events in the correct order.

_____ The Stowe family moves to Maine.

_____ *Uncle Tom's Cabin* is published.

_____ Stowe's son dies of cholera.

_____ Harriet Beecher marries Calvin Stowe.

_____ Stowe travels in Europe.

_____ Stowe meets President Lincoln.

Vocabulary

Look at these words from the reading. Put a check next to words that you know. Underline words that you don't know yet. Find the words in the reading. Try to guess their meanings.

abolitionists	cholera	grief	progressive
advocated	fugitive	inhumanity	

Use the words to fill in the blanks in the story.

Harriet Beecher's family encouraged discussions about _____ social
1

ideas. Harriet met Calvin Stowe at a club, and they married in 1836.

At that time, slavery was an important issue. The Stowes were _____
2

who believed that slavery was wrong. When their son died from _____,
3

Harriet was filled with _____. The family moved to Maine, and Stowe
4

began writing about social issues. She wrote an article about the

sufferings of _____ slaves. Later, she wrote her most famous book, *Uncle*
5

Tom's Cabin. She wanted to show the _____ of slavery. *Uncle Tom's*
6

Cabin quickly became a best seller. Stowe traveled widely discussing

the book. After slavery became illegal, she _____ civil rights for blacks
7

and voting rights for women.

Reading a Chart

A chart is a useful way to organize facts.

Some Famous Abolitionists

Name	Birthplace	Born	Died	Key Facts and Events
Lucretia Mott	Nantucket, Massachusetts	1793	1880	A Quaker minister. To protest slavery, she boycotted cotton and sugar cane because slaves farmed those crops.
John Brown	Torrington, Connecticut	1800	1859	He stole guns to help slaves fight slave owners. He was caught and hanged for treason.
Harriet Tubman	Maryland	1830	1913	A former slave. She risked her life on the Underground Railroad to help more than 300 slaves get to freedom.
Charlotte Forten	Philadelphia, Pennsylvania	1837	1914	A prominent wealthy black woman. Her family financed at least six antislavery groups.

Answer the questions. Use information from the chart.

1. Which famous abolitionist came from an important black family?

   _____

2. Why was John Brown hanged? What did he do? _____

   _____

3. How did Harriet Tubman risk her life many times? _____

   _____

4. How did Lucretia Mott protest slavery? _____

   _____

Discuss: What type of people were these abolitionists? How were they alike? How were they different?

Connecting Today and Yesterday

1. During Stowe's life, people got news from newspapers, books, magazines, conversations, and speeches. How do we get our news today? Which way is best? Explain.

2. Catherine Beecher ran a school for girls. Why did boys and girls go to school separately then? Why do they go to school together today? Which way do you think is better? Explain.

Group Activities

1. Research the abolitionist movement in the United States. When did it begin? How did abolitionists try to end slavery? How effective were they?

2. Imagine that you are an abolitionist who helped a fugitive slave. Write a page in your diary about how you helped the slave. Explain why you did it. Share your story with the class.

Class Discussion

1. Describe the Fugitive Slave Act. Why were abolitionists angry about it?

2. Why did Stowe decide to write *Uncle Tom's Cabin?* What did she say about her reasons?

3. How did Stowe describe blacks in *Uncle Tom's Cabin?*

4. Why did Abraham Lincoln call Stowe "the little lady who . . . started this Great War"? Do you think that a book can influence history?

Reflections

1. What was the most interesting thing that you read in this lesson?

2. Can you use anything from Harriet Beecher Stowe's story in your own life? Explain.

3. How can you learn more about Harriet Beecher Stowe or *Uncle Tom's Cabin?*

Walt Whitman

*"One's heart grows sick of war . . .
when you see what it really is."*

—Walt Whitman[1]

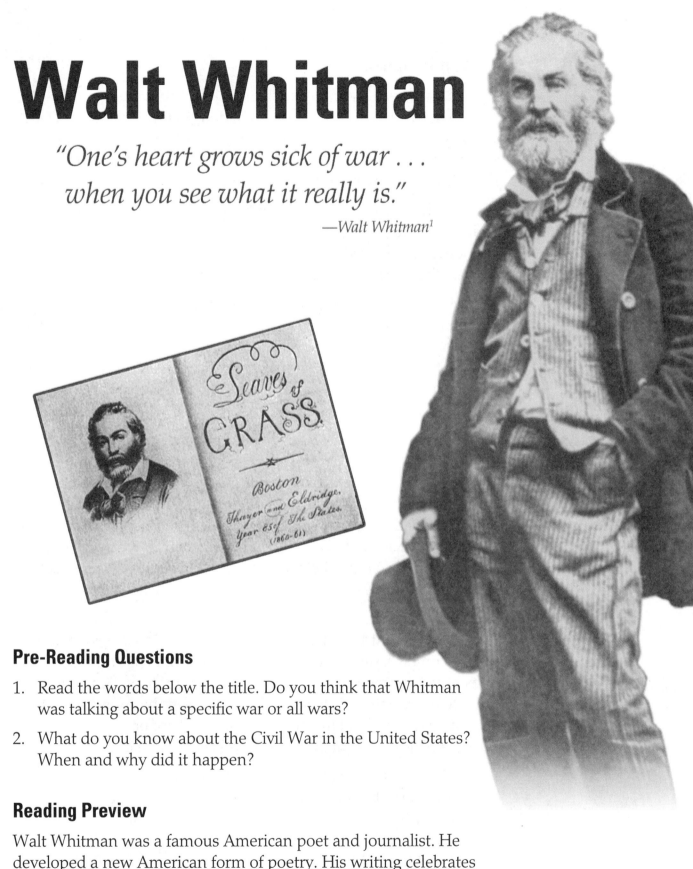

Pre-Reading Questions

1. Read the words below the title. Do you think that Whitman was talking about a specific war or all wars?

2. What do you know about the Civil War in the United States? When and why did it happen?

Reading Preview

Walt Whitman was a famous American poet and journalist. He developed a new American form of poetry. His writing celebrates the American spirit. During the Civil War, Whitman took care of wounded soldiers. From that experience, he learned about the terrible conditions of the war. He wrote movingly about the suffering it caused.

Walt Whitman

Walt Whitman's family had lived in America since the early 1600s. His parents taught their children to love American ideals. They expressed their patriotism by giving three of their sons the names of presidents—George Washington Whitman, Andrew Jackson Whitman, and Thomas Jefferson Whitman.

While growing up, Whitman heard his parents' progressive ideas. He learned their liberal ways of thinking. Whitman's mother introduced him to Quaker philosophy. Quakers oppose war. This pacifism influenced Whitman greatly later in his life.

Whitman attended public schools until he was 11 years old. Then he began working as an office clerk for a group of lawyers. On this job, he could borrow books from a nearby library. In this way, he satisfied his great interest in people and ideas. Whitman continued his self-education by visiting museums. He also spoke to everyone he met about the important political issues of the day.

In 1831, Whitman became a newspaper apprentice. He worked at the *Long Island Patriot.* There, he learned the skill of printing. He also discovered the joy of putting words into print. At age 14, he had his first article printed in the paper. Later, he took a job at a Louisiana newspaper. This was his first time in a state where slavery was legal. In New Orleans, Whitman saw slaves being bought and sold just below his hotel window. The sight upset him greatly. In later years, he wrote about the need to end slavery.

When he left Louisiana, Whitman returned to Brooklyn and lived on his family's farm. He began to develop a new form of poetry. Whitman believed that the new nation needed a new form of writing. This new writing expressed the American belief in individuality and freedom. His new style of poetry was free verse. This style sounded like people talking or singing.

Whitman's poems often dealt with patriotic topics. Many poems were about the spirit of the American people and individual expression. Whitman also wrote openly about the human body. In 1855 he published his poetry in a book called *Leaves of Grass.* Many people loved Whitman's work because it was a new American voice. Other people didn't like it because it didn't follow the traditional rules of poetry in English.

Whitman's *Leaves of Grass* was about a unified nation. But during the 1850s, there were serious disagreements between the North and the South. Southern states complained that federal laws benefited only the northern states. The northern economy was based on manufacturing. The southern economy was based mostly on farming. In the South, cotton and tobacco were grown on large plantations. These plantations depended on slave labor. But people in many northern states wanted the South to end slavery.

Seven southern states decided to create their own government. They seceded, or left the United States. They called their new government the Confederacy. President Abraham Lincoln believed that it was illegal for these states to separate from the United States. Then Confederate soldiers fired shots at a federal fort, Fort Sumter, in South Carolina on April 12, 1861. Four more southern states seceded and joined the Confederacy. The Civil War had begun.

The northern, or Union, army fought to end slavery. It fought to bring all the states together again. The Confederacy wanted to remain separate and to keep slavery. Most people expected a short war, but the Civil War was long and bloody. It lasted four years. More than 500,000 men were killed.[2] This is the largest number of U.S. deaths in any war.

After the battle of Fredericksburg, Virginia, Whitman saw his brother George's name on a list of casualties. Whitman went to Washington, D.C., to find his brother in the hospital. Fortunately, his brother was not seriously hurt. But outside the hospital, Whitman saw badly wounded soldiers. Doctors had amputated the arms or legs of many of them.

Whitman looked for a way that he could help. He began to assist doctors during surgeries, a skill that he had learned in New York. He also offered friendship to the wounded soldiers. He wrote letters and did errands for them. And he tried to comfort and support them. Whitman worked many long hours every day to help these men. He hoped that his work could help heal the country. For four years, he wrote a daily diary of his experiences in war hospitals in both the North and the South. He later wrote a book of emotional poems called *Drum-Taps.* These poems

"The wounded . . . arrive at the rate of 1,000 a day."

—*Walt Whitman, writing from Chancellorsville, Virginia*[3]

spoke of the terrible conditions during the Civil War and the high number of casualties.

After the war, Whitman stayed in Washington and worked for the Department of the Interior. This job helped support his writing. He also got help from other writers. In 1873, on a visit to his mother and brother in Camden, New Jersey, he had a stroke and lost some of his ability to move. He remained in Camden and continued to write. Whitman died in Camden on March 26, 1892, at age 73. His writing influenced the work of many future American and international writers.

Comprehension

Complete the sentences. Use information from the reading.

1. When Whitman was growing up, his mother taught him _____

   _____.

2. At the *Long Island Patriot*, Whitman learned _____

   _____.

3. When Whitman saw slaves being bought and sold, he felt _____

   _____.

4. Whitman developed a new style of poetry that expressed _____

   _____.

5. In the 1850s, there were conflicts between the North and

   South because _____

   _____.

6. The southern states seceded because _____

   _____.

7. When Whitman visited a military hospital, he _____

   _____.

8. Whitman wrote *Drum-Taps* because _____

   _____.

Sequence

Work with a partner. Number the events in the correct order.

_____ Whitman begins helping wounded soldiers.

_____ Whitman begins writing a new style of poetry.

_____ Whitman publishes *Leaves of Grass.*

_____ Whitman writes *Drum-Taps.*

_____ Seven southern states form the Confederacy.

Vocabulary

Look at these words from the reading. Put a check next to words that you know. Underline words that you don't know yet. Find the words in the reading. Try to guess their meanings.

amputate	casualties	individuality	patriotic
apprentice	errand	pacifism	secede

Check the correct meaning for each word.

1. pacifism

   _____ a. religious belief

   _____ b. desire to write

   _____ c. opposition to war

2. apprentice

   _____ a. teacher

   _____ b. trainee

   _____ c. writer

3. individuality

   _____ a. unique personality

   _____ b. federal government

   _____ c. independence

4. patriotic

   _____ a. showing love of country

   _____ b. showing need for slavery

   _____ c. showing love of children

5. secede

   _____ a. to leave

   _____ b. to enroll

   _____ c. to visit

6. amputate

   _____ a. to bandage

   _____ b. to add on

   _____ c. to cut off

7. errand

   _____ a. a talk to cheer someone up

   _____ b. a short trip to do something

   _____ c. washing someone's clothes

8. casualties

   _____ a. dead or wounded people

   _____ b. groups of soldiers

   _____ c. reasons for a war

Walt Whitman **43**

Reading a Map

Physical maps show features of land and water. **Political maps** show borders between countries, states, or other organized territories. **Historical maps** show features from the past. Some maps, like this one, combine all three types. It shows physical and political features of the United States during the Civil War. States that seceded formed the Confederacy. The remaining states, plus the territories, were the Union.

The United States in the Civil War

Answer the questions. Use information from the map.

1. How many states were in the Confederacy? _____

2. The Civil War started on April 12, 1861. Which states joined
   the Confederacy after the war started? _____

   _____

3. Which slave states did not join the Confederacy? _____

   _____

4. How many Union states were there in the Civil War? _____

5. Which had more land area, the Union or the Confederacy? _____

Connecting Today and Yesterday

1. Since the Civil War, American photographers have taken pictures of soldiers and battles. Do you think that people should be allowed to photograph everything that happens in a war? Why or why not?

2. When Whitman published his first book, *Leaves of Grass,* many people didn't like his new form of writing. Today, however, Whitman's poetry is very popular. Can you think of other times when something new was not accepted at first, but later became popular?

Group Activities

1. Get a copy of Whitman's *Leaves of Grass.* Choose a poem from the book to share with your group. Read the poem out loud. Does it sound like someone talking or singing? Choose three lines from the poem and discuss their meaning.

2. Do you like Whitman's style? Why or why not? Why were some people surprised by Whitman's new style of poetry? What kind of poetry do you like to read? Bring a copy of a poem you like to class and share it with your group.

Class Discussion

1. How did Whitman demonstrate his interest in self-education?

2. How were Whitman's life and writing influenced by his parents' patriotism and liberal ideas?

3. What did Whitman do to help wounded soldiers? Why did he help them?

4. If Lincoln had allowed the Confederacy to secede, what might have happened to the United States? What would the country be like today?

Reflections

1. What was the most interesting thing that you read in this lesson?

2. Can you use anything from Walt Whitman's story in your own life? Explain.

3. How can you learn more about Walt Whitman or the Civil War?

Whitman said, "The United States themselves are essentially the greatest poem."[4]

What did he mean? How did he show this belief in his life?

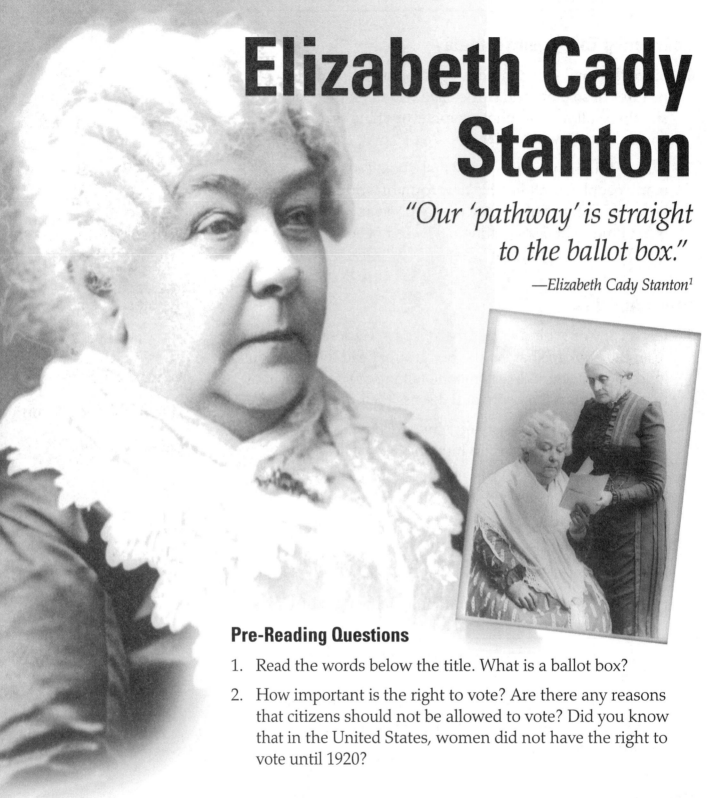

Elizabeth Cady Stanton

"Our 'pathway' is straight to the ballot box."

—Elizabeth Cady Stanton[1]

Pre-Reading Questions

1. Read the words below the title. What is a ballot box?

2. How important is the right to vote? Are there any reasons that citizens should not be allowed to vote? Did you know that in the United States, women did not have the right to vote until 1920?

Reading Preview

Elizabeth Cady Stanton wanted to improve women's lives. She wanted women to be able to vote and get a good education. Stanton was one of the first people in the United States to focus on women's voting rights. She helped bring this issue to public attention. She worked hard to change U.S. voting laws.

Elizabeth Cady Stanton

Elizabeth Cady was born in 1815 in Johnstown, New York. Her parents were well-to-do and sent her to the best private schools. She was an excellent student and an independent thinker. After graduating, she studied law in her father's office. She learned that the legal system was unfair to women.

In 1840, Elizabeth Cady married Henry Brewster Stanton. He was a lawyer and abolitionist who shared her political views. They spent their honeymoon in London at the World Anti-Slavery Conference. At this conference, the women delegates could not sit with the men. They were not allowed to speak. This treatment made Stanton angry. She was determined to work for women's equality.

At this time, women had almost no legal rights in the United States. Most women couldn't get a good education. If they married, their property belonged to their husbands. If a wife earned a salary, the money belonged to her husband. In a divorce, a woman had no right to custody of her children.

In 1847, Stanton and her husband moved to Seneca Falls, New York. There she began to work with Lucretia Mott, an activist in the antislavery movement. They planned the first women's rights convention in the United States. This event happened in Seneca Falls in 1848. More than 300 women attended. At the convention, Stanton presented a paper called "A Declaration of Sentiments." This paper listed laws that showed the inferior legal status of women.

Stanton also wrote several resolutions for the convention. These resolutions said that women needed rights at home and in the courts. Most delegates agreed with these ideas. But one resolution called for women's suffrage, or voting rights. Many delegates refused to sign that resolution. They were afraid that men, including their husbands, would laugh at them.

Many newspapers ran cartoons that ridiculed women's fight for legal rights. Some women felt embarrassed that they had signed the resolutions. However, Stanton was confident. She wrote to every newspaper that had ridiculed women. Her letters brought the issue to everyone's attention.

In 1851, Stanton met Susan B. Anthony, and one of the great partnerships in the women's movement began. Anthony was a

> *"We hold these truths to be self-evident: that all men and women are created equal."*
>
> —Elizabeth Cady Stanton[2]

Quaker and an abolitionist. She and Stanton worked together for 50 years. Anthony was not married, so she could travel. She spoke to many women's groups. She organized women to fight for their rights. Stanton needed to care for her seven children at home. So she wrote speeches, articles, and letters. Anthony used those writings in the fight for women's rights.

As one of their first projects, Stanton and Anthony worked to change the New York Married Women's Property Law. This law took away a married woman's salary and custody of her children in a divorce. In an unusual action, the New York state legislature invited Stanton to speak in 1854. She convinced the legislature to change the law. Beginning in 1860, a married woman in New York state had the right to keep her own salary. And she had an equal right to have custody of her children.

In 1870, the 15th Amendment became part of the U.S. Constitution. This amendment gave black men the right to vote. But the Constitution still did not allow women to vote. In 1878, Stanton wrote an amendment to give voting rights to women. Every year for 39 years, this proposed amendment was introduced in Congress, but it was not passed.

Stanton and Anthony continued their fight. In 1890, they helped merge two strong women's organizations and formed the National American Woman Suffrage Organization. They also changed some of their strategies. They knew that the states would have to ratify, or approve, a suffrage amendment after it passed in Congress. If three-fourths of the states ratified the amendment, it would become part of the Constitution. So Anthony and Stanton worked on building support inside each state.

In the 1890s, Stanton moved to New York City. There, she continued her fight for women's rights. She died of heart failure in 1902, two weeks before her 87th birthday.

Stanton didn't live to see voting rights for women. But she inspired many younger women, including her daughter, Harriet Stanton Blatch. These women continued Stanton's fight for suffrage.

Stanton's suffrage amendment was passed in Congress on August 26, 1919. The 19th Amendment was ratified by three-fourths of the states one year later. All Americans, women and men of all races, now had the right to vote.

Comprehension

Check the correct answer.

1. Elizabeth Cady's family

    _____ a. sent her to a good school.

    _____ b. tutored her at home.

    _____ c. was not interested in educating her.

2. Elizabeth Cady first became interested in women's rights

    _____ a. when she met Lucretia Mott.

    _____ b. in London at the World Anti-Slavery Convention.

    _____ c. when she studied law in her father's office.

3. In the early 1800s, women in the U.S. had few rights

    _____ a. and all their property belonged to their husbands.

    _____ b. and they couldn't keep their own last names.

    _____ c. and they were not allowed to work.

4. When the women's rights convention called for suffrage,

    _____ a. many women feared a negative reaction.

    _____ b. many newspapers also supported suffrage.

    _____ c. Stanton was not confident about the issue.

5. Stanton and Anthony had a good partnership because

    _____ a. Anthony taught Stanton about abolition.

    _____ b. Anthony could travel, so Stanton could stay home with her children.

    _____ c. Stanton spoke poorly, so Anthony gave speeches.

6. The 15th Amendment

    _____ a. gave all black people the right to vote.

    _____ b. gave all women the right to vote.

    _____ c. gave black men the right to vote.

7. The 19th Amendment had to be ratified

    _____ a. by all the states.

    _____ b. by the president.

    _____ c. by three-fourths of the states.

Sequence

Work with a partner. Number the events in the correct order.

_____ Stanton begins a partnership with Susan B. Anthony.

_____ Elizabeth Cady marries Henry Brewster Stanton.

_____ Stanton speaks to the New York state legislature about the Married Women's Property Law.

_____ The 19th Amendment is ratified.

_____ The National American Woman Suffrage Organization is formed.

_____ The women's rights convention takes place in Seneca Falls.

Vocabulary

Look at these words from the reading. Put a check next to words that you know. Underline words that you don't know yet. Find the words in the reading. Try to guess their meanings.

activist	ratified	ridiculed	suffrage
delegates	resolutions	status	well-to-do

Use the words to fill in the blanks in the story.

Elizabeth Cady Stanton came from a _____ family. When she

learned about the inferior legal _____ of women, she became

an _____ for women's rights. At the Seneca Falls convention for

women's rights, the _____ passed many _____,

including one supporting women's _____. Many men and newspapers

_____ women's rights. Even so, an amendment giving women the right

to vote was finally _____ in 1920.

Reading a Time Line

A time line shows dates and events in order on a line.

Events in the History of Women's Rights

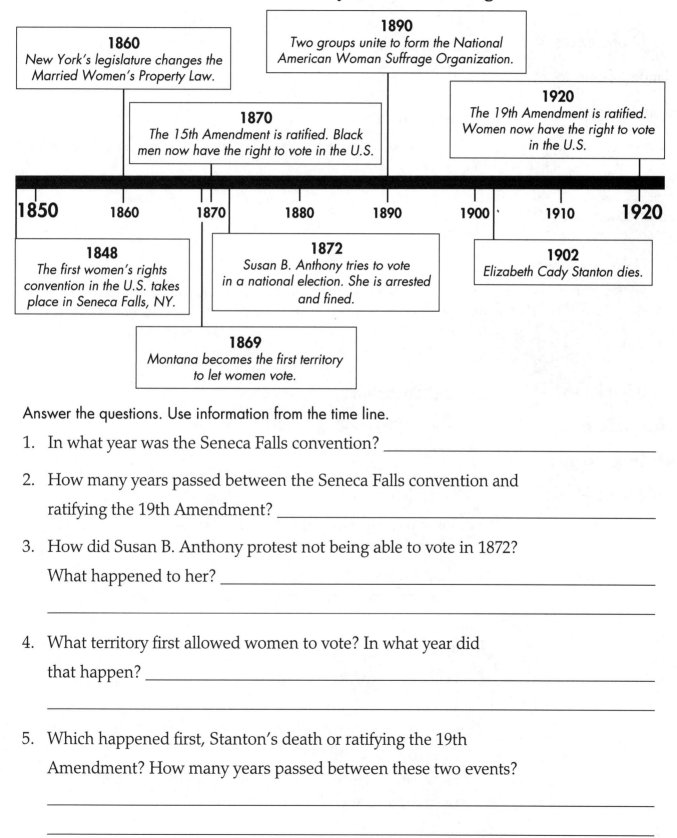

1860
New York's legislature changes the Married Women's Property Law.

1890
Two groups unite to form the National American Woman Suffrage Organization.

1870
The 15th Amendment is ratified. Black men now have the right to vote in the U.S.

1920
The 19th Amendment is ratified. Women now have the right to vote in the U.S.

1850   1860   1870   1880   1890   1900   1910   1920

1848
The first women's rights convention in the U.S. takes place in Seneca Falls, NY.

1872
Susan B. Anthony tries to vote in a national election. She is arrested and fined.

1902
Elizabeth Cady Stanton dies.

1869
Montana becomes the first territory to let women vote.

Answer the questions. Use information from the time line.

1. In what year was the Seneca Falls convention? _____

2. How many years passed between the Seneca Falls convention and ratifying the 19th Amendment? _____

3. How did Susan B. Anthony protest not being able to vote in 1872? What happened to her? _____

_____

4. What territory first allowed women to vote? In what year did that happen? _____

_____

5. Which happened first, Stanton's death or ratifying the 19th Amendment? How many years passed between these two events?

_____

_____

> "The right of citizens of the United States to vote shall not be denied [taken away] or abridged [limited] . . . on account of sex."
>
> —19th Amendment (ratified August 18, 1920)

Why did it take so long for women in the United States to gain the right to vote?

Connecting Today and Yesterday

1. In your community, what issues are important to women? How are these issues like the issues in the 1800s? How are they different?

2. How do newspapers and TV treat women's issues today? Is this treatment like or unlike newspaper coverage in the 1800s?

Group Activity

With your group, write three questions about the changes in women's role in society:

1. _____

2. _____

3. _____

Think of women that you know. Pick women from two or three different generations. Ask them your questions. Write their responses on separate paper. Share the responses with your group. Which generation saw the most changes? Explain.

Class Discussion

1. What obstacles did women face in their fight for voting rights?

2. Why was the 15th Amendment passed before the 19th Amendment?

3. Some western territories and states allowed women to vote before 1920. Why did they do that?

4. Suppose you wanted community support for a project benefiting women. What strategies would you use?

Reflections

1. What was the most interesting thing that you read in this lesson?

2. Can you use anything from Elizabeth Cady Stanton's story in your own life? Explain.

3. How can you learn more about Elizabeth Cady Stanton or the women's movement in the United States?

Eugene V. Debs

"Am I my brother's keeper? . . .
Yes, I am my brother's keeper."

—Eugene V. Debs[1]

Pre-Reading Questions

1. Read the words below the title. Do you know where they
    come from? What do they mean? Who do you think that
    Debs meant when he said "my brother"?

2. What should the relationship be like between workers and
    business owners? Should workers have a right to go on strike
    against a company? Why or why not?

Reading Preview

Eugene Debs was an active union organizer. He fought bravely
for changes in labor laws. He helped workers win new rights.
Many of these changes are now important in the life of every
worker in the United States.

Eugene V. Debs

One of Eugene Debs's best childhood memories was Sunday evenings. His father read books aloud to the children. Debs especially remembered *Les Miserables* by Victor Hugo. The hero, Jean Valjean, has to steal bread to feed his family. This story ignited Debs's interest in the rights of workers.

Debs was born on November 5, 1855, in Terre Haute, Indiana. His parents had immigrated to the United States from Colmar, France. They ran a successful grocery store in the front of their house. Although Debs did well in school, he felt restless. He left school when he was 14 years old and started working for the railroad as a paint scraper. Later, he became a locomotive fireman. But he traveled long distances, and his parents worried about his safety. So he took a job in his hometown. He worked for a wholesale grocery company. He also took business classes in the evenings.

During this time, Debs became active in the Occidental Literary Society. This progressive group invited speakers on many issues. Debs participated in debates at meetings. He gained experience as a public speaker.

At the railroad, Debs had seen much injustice toward workers. Changes in manufacturing had made the workers poor. In the early 1800s, manufacturing companies had usually been small businesses. The owners knew the workers by name. These owners generally treated workers well.

But in Debs's time, small manufacturers were disappearing. A complex system was replacing them. This system, including the railroads, used modern machines. It required many workers. But many business owners cared only about profits. They exploited the workers. Some workers worked 12 to 16 hours a day, seven days a week. They generally didn't get any benefits, such as insurance or death benefits.

In the mid-1870s, Debs joined the Brotherhood of Locomotive Firemen. He soon became recording secretary of his local chapter. He also worked as an organizer. He urged railroad workers to join the union.

Debs wrote popular articles about workers' rights in the union magazine. He became well-known for his labor work. He was also known for his powerful speeches in support of workers.

Debs was elected to the Indiana General Assembly in 1884. But he became disappointed in politics. After his term ended, he decided to work full-time as a labor organizer.

Debs believed that railroad workers should have one large union instead of many smaller ones. He believed that one large union would give the workers more power. In 1893, Debs successfully merged all the unions into the American Railway Union. It was the first industrial union in the United States, and Debs was its first president. Under Debs's leadership, this union gained national attention in April 1894. It conducted a successful strike against the Great Northern Railway. After 18 days, the owners agreed to pay higher wages. They also agreed to improve working conditions.

Debs led the union in another strike later in 1894. It was supporting workers who were on strike against the Pullman Palace Car Company. It tied up the entire U.S. railroad system. In Chicago, 5,000 union supporters demonstrated. President Grover Cleveland called out the army to disperse, or chase away, the demonstrators. The army arrested 700 people and shot 13 to death. Attorney General Richard Olney got an injunction, or court order. The injunction said that the strike was illegal. But Debs refused to stop the strike. He was arrested and put in jail for six months.

Debs was upset by the government's actions. In jail, he thought about how to create a more equal society. He decided that government should own the industries.

When he left jail, Debs decided to work for a socialist government in the United States. He helped found, or start, the Social Democratic Party. Debs urged Americans to use their votes to create a new government. In 1900, he was the party's first candidate for president. His platform called for making workplaces safer, allowing women to vote, and restricting child labor. Debs also wanted workers to be able to join unions.

William McKinley won the 1900 presidential election. But Debs continued to build support for his ideas. In 1901, the Social Democratic Party merged with the Socialist Labor Party. They formed the Socialist Party of America. By the 1904 presidential election, the Socialist Party had grown. It was the third largest party in the United States. Debs ran for president as a Socialist in 1904, 1908, 1912, and 1920. He was defeated each time. But in

"While there is a lower class, I am in it, . . . and while there is a soul in prison, I am not free."

—*Eugene V. Debs*[2]

1920, he received almost a million votes—even though he was in prison for making an antiwar speech.

Debs's hard work and constant travel affected his health. Twice he entered the Lindlahr Sanitarium in Elmhurst, Illinois, to recover from stress. Even in the hospital, he remained active in the socialist movement. He died in October 1926. A statue of Debs in the Labor Hall of Fame in Washington, D.C., honors him for his labor work.

Comprehension

Complete the sentences. Use information from the reading.

1. One of Debs's favorite childhood memories was _____
   _____.

2. In the Occidental Literary Society, Debs _____
   _____.

3. Debs began to support labor when he _____
   _____.

4. Debs wanted one large union of railroad workers because _____
   _____.

5. The 1894 Pullman strike became violent when _____
   _____.

6. When he was in prison after the Pullman strike, Debs _____
   _____.

7. When Debs ran for president in 1900, his platform included _____
   _____.

8. Many people call Debs a hero of the American labor movement
   because _____.

Sequence

Work with a partner. Number the events in the correct order.

_____ Debs runs for president for the first time.

_____ Debs supports the Pullman strike.

_____ Debs joins the Brotherhood of Locomotive Firemen.

_____ Debs works as a paint scraper.

_____ Debs goes to jail for the first time.

Vocabulary

Look at these words from the reading. Put a check next to words that you know. Underline words that you don't know yet. Find the words in the reading. Try to guess their meanings.

disperse	found	injunction	platform
exploit	ignite	merge	tie up

Check the correct meaning for each word.

1. ignite
   _____ a. to start
   _____ b. to turn off
   _____ c. to move away

2. exploit
   _____ a. to discover
   _____ b. to sell overseas
   _____ c. to use selfishly

3. merge
   _____ a. to drive a car
   _____ b. to join together
   _____ c. to turn around

4. tie up
   _____ a. to wrap a package
   _____ b. to prevent movement
   _____ c. to cause progress

5. disperse
   _____ a. to collect money
   _____ b. to chase away
   _____ c. to give away

6. injunction
   _____ a. arrest
   _____ b. court order
   _____ c. place on a map

7. found
   _____ a. to return
   _____ b. to start
   _____ c. to move forward

8. platform
   _____ a. plan for government
   _____ b. election
   _____ c. voters

Reading a Chart

A chart is a useful way to organize facts.

Inventions That Changed the United States

Name of Inventor	Year	Invention
Western Union Company	1856	a system of telegraph wires that connected the whole country
Isaac Singer	1860	an easy-to-use sewing machine
Christopher Sholes	1867	the typewriter
Thomas Edison	1877	the phonograph
	1879	a practical electric lightbulb
	1891	the motion picture camera
Orville and Wilbur Wright	1903	the airplane

How do you think that each new invention contributed to U.S. industries? What could people do that they couldn't do before? Think about these questions. Then complete the sentences with your ideas.

1. Electric lights permitted people to _____
   _____.

2. The sewing machine changed the way _____
   _____.

3. When people could type, _____
   _____.

4. The ability to fly allowed people to _____
   _____.

5. Because people could send a telegram anywhere in the country, _____
   _____.

Discuss: In your opinion, which invention listed here was the most important? Explain.

Connecting Today and Yesterday

1. How have working conditions changed in the United States since the early 1900s? What benefits can workers get today?

2. Do U.S. workers still need any changes in their working conditions? If so, what changes do they need? Why?

Group Activity

List three problems that workers face today. Then write a solution for each problem. Discuss your answers.

Problem	Solution
1. _____	1. _____
2. _____	2. _____
3. _____	3. _____

Class Discussion

1. What influences in Debs's early life made him interested in workers' rights?

2. How did Debs contribute to the development of railroad unions?

3. In the early 1900s, what were working conditions like in U.S. industries?

4. The Socialist Party was popular in the 1920s. But it never won a national election. Why? Explain your opinion.

5. Debs thought that the U.S. government should own the industries. He believed that would make society more equal. Do you agree or disagree? Do you think that a more equal society is possible? Explain.

Reflections

1. What was the most interesting thing that you read in this lesson?

2. Can you use anything from Eugene Debs's story in your own life? Explain.

3. How can you learn more about Eugene Debs or the socialist movement in the United States?

Debs opposed war. When the United States got involved in World War I, he protested. In 1918, he was sentenced to 10 years in prison for his protest.

Was it right to put him in prison for his beliefs? Why or why not?

Dorothea Lange

"A picture is worth a thousand words."

—*well-known saying*

Pre-Reading Questions

1. Look at the words below the title. What do you think that they mean? Do you agree or disagree?

2. Has a photograph ever made you think about something in a new way? If so, what photograph was it? How did it influence you?

Reading Preview

Dorothea Lange helped create the art of documentary photography. Her photos were realistic and emotional. They showed the effects of the Great Depression on ordinary Americans.

Dorothea Lange

Dorothea Lange was born in Hoboken, New Jersey, in 1895. When she was seven, she got polio. From this disease, she developed a limp in one leg. She said that this disability made her more sensitive to the sufferings of other people. Her later photos clearly expressed her feelings for others.

When Lange was still a child, she and her mother moved to New York City. She often walked around the city, watching people.

Lange graduated from high school in 1913. To please her mother, she enrolled in a teacher-training program. But she really dreamed of being a photographer. One day Lange was passing the photography shop of Arnold Genthe. She went inside and asked for a job. Genthe hired her as an assistant.

In Genthe's shop, Lange learned darkroom techniques and portrait photography. She dropped out of the teacher-training program. Instead, she enrolled in a photography class. At the end of the class, she bought her first large camera and two lenses. Lange began to photograph relatives and friends. She converted a chicken coop in her backyard into a darkroom. There, she developed her pictures.

In 1918, Lange moved to San Francisco. She got a job as a photo finisher and joined the Camera Club. She also met her first husband, Western wilderness painter Maynard Dixon. Soon Lange opened her own photography studio. Over the next 10 years, she became a successful portrait photographer for wealthy San Franciscans.

On October 29, 1929, the U.S. stock market collapsed. That was the start of the Great Depression. Banks failed and businesses closed. Millions of people lost their jobs. Many were homeless and had little to eat. The federal government had few programs to help them. There was no relief for their suffering.

Some areas of the country were especially devastated. In those areas, the weather made the effects of the Depression worse. Parts of Kansas, Oklahoma, Texas, New Mexico, and Colorado were called the Dust Bowl. Terrible dust storms and drought forced people to abandon their farms. They packed their few possessions into broken-down cars and left their homes. Many drove to California. There they hoped to find work as migrant farm workers. One preacher said, "The land just blew away; we had to go somewhere."[1]

Lange was moved by these migrant families as they drove through San Francisco. In 1933, Lange photographed a man in tattered clothing waiting in line for food. She called this photograph "White Angel Breadline," and it became famous. Lange realized that she was not just photographing a man. She was also telling about his life. Lange then began to use her photographs to document the Depression.

In 1934, Lange met Paul Taylor, an economics professor, at an exhibit of her work. California's Rural Rehabilitation Agency had asked Taylor to study the conditions of migrant farm workers in the state. Taylor invited Lange to work as a photographer in the study. Lange agreed.

Throughout the study, Taylor and Lange interviewed their subjects before Lange photographed them. This practice helped create intimate pictures. The study provided compelling interviews and photographs. Because of their work, California set up several programs to help migrant workers.

Lange and Dixon divorced in 1935, and Lange married Taylor. She and Taylor began working for the Farm Security Agency, or FSA. This federal agency helped unemployed and homeless people. Lange traveled throughout the country. She photographed people and their living conditions in 22 states.

Lange took her most famous photograph in 1936. The photo, "Migrant Mother," shows a 32-year-old mother with her children. They were in a camp for migrant pea-pickers in California. The family lived in an open tent. The peas had frozen on the vines, so there was no work. They survived by eating the frozen peas and birds that the children caught. They could not go somewhere else because the mother had sold their car tires to buy food. Lange's photo captured this woman's story. It was printed around the country. As a result, the federal government immediately sent 20,000 pounds of food to the pea-picker camp.

Lange worked for the FSA for 14 years. Later, she traveled around the world taking pictures. She advanced the art of documentary photography. And through her success, she opened the door for women photographers. Lange died of cancer in 1965, but her photos still tell their stories.

Comprehension

Check the correct answer.

1. Lange said that polio

_____ a. made her more sensitive to other people.

_____ b. was not important in her life.

_____ c. made her feel depressed.

2. After Lange enrolled in a teacher-training course, she

_____ a. soon got her teaching certificate.

_____ b. began teaching high school students.

_____ c. dropped out and took a photography class.

3. When Lange moved to San Francisco, she

_____ a. opened her own photography shop.

_____ b. worked only for other photographers.

_____ c. photographed the western wilderness.

4. During the Great Depression, many people in the Dust Bowl

_____ a. made their livings as business owners.

_____ b. left their farms and became migrant workers.

_____ c. had no problems.

5. Before Lange photographed someone,

_____ a. she and Taylor interviewed the person.

_____ b. she posed the person.

_____ c. she talked about her own life.

6. The Farm Security Agency

_____ a. did not help farmers.

_____ b. was a state agency.

_____ c. helped homeless and unemployed people.

7. Lange is called a documentary photographer because

_____ a. she wrote stories about her photographs.

_____ b. her photographs documented a person's story.

_____ c. her photographs were on TV.

Sequence

Work with a partner. Number the events in the correct order.

_____ Lange graduates from high school.

_____ Lange sets up a darkroom at home.

_____ Lange gets polio.

_____ The U.S. stock market collapses.

_____ Lange begins to work for the Farm Security Agency.

_____ Lange publishes the photograph "Migrant Mother."

Vocabulary

Look at these words from the reading. Put a check next to words that you know. Underline words that you don't know yet. Find the words in the reading. Try to guess their meanings.

abandon	devastated	intimate	polio
converted	drought	limp	portrait

Use the words to fill in the blanks in the story.

As a child, Lange developed _____ and walked with a
                                          1
_____. She was interested in observing the world, and she began
              2

taking photographs. She developed her pictures in a chicken coop

that she _____ into a darkroom. She later moved to San Francisco and
                    3

became well-known for her _____ photography. During the Great
                                      4

Depression, she photographed migrant workers. Many of these

people had lived in Oklahoma and nearby states, but a _____ had
                                                                        5

created a Dust Bowl there. The land was _____ , and the people had to
                                                        6

_____ their farms. Lange's _____ photographs showed
              7   8

the personal effects of these hard times.

Reading a Time Line

A time line shows dates and events in order on a line.

The Dust Bowl: 1931–1939

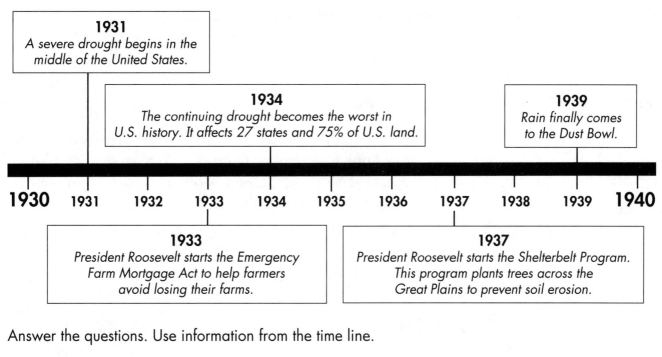

1931
A severe drought begins in the middle of the United States.

1934
The continuing drought becomes the worst in U.S. history. It affects 27 states and 75% of U.S. land.

1939
Rain finally comes to the Dust Bowl.

1930 1931 1932 1933 1934 1935 1936 1937 1938 1939 1940

1933
President Roosevelt starts the Emergency Farm Mortgage Act to help farmers avoid losing their farms.

1937
President Roosevelt starts the Shelterbelt Program. This program plants trees across the Great Plains to prevent soil erosion.

Answer the questions. Use information from the time line.

1. How many years did the drought last? _____

2. How many states were affected by the drought? _____

3. How much U.S. land was affected by the drought? _____

4. When did the Emergency Farm Mortgage Act take effect?
   What did it do? _____

   _____

5. When did the Shelterbelt Program start? What did it do? _____

   _____

Discuss: Should the government provide help in a natural disaster like a drought? What kind of help?

Dorothea Lange was called "a missionary of change."[3]

Do you agree? Why or why not?

Connecting Today and Yesterday

1. Have you seen a news photograph that could influence public opinion? What was the photograph? What was your reaction?

2. Lange's photographs educated people about social issues of her time. What should the role of photographers be in dealing with social issues?

Group Activities

1. Find photographs by Dorothea Lange in the library or on the Internet. Look for the photographs "White Angel Breadline" and "Migrant Mother," as well as others. What do you like about them? Is there anything that you don't like? Explain.

2. As a class, watch the movie *The Grapes of Wrath,* based on a book by John Steinbeck. Why did Steinbeck and Lange want to show the lives of migrant workers during the Depression?

Class Discussion

1. How did Lange's early life influence her photography?

2. How did Lange pursue her interest in photography when she was young?

3. What were some of the effects of the Great Depression? What did the government do to help people?

4. How did Lange and Taylor try to make Lange's photographs more effective?

5. How did Lange's photographs change U.S. society?

Reflections

1. What was the most interesting thing that you read in this lesson?

2. Can you use anything from Dorothea Lange's story in your own life? Explain.

3. How can you learn more about Dorothea Lange or the Great Depression?

Felix Frankfurter

It is the duty of a judge "not to act merely on personal views."

—Felix Frankfurter[1]

Pre-Reading Questions

1. Read the words below the title. What do you think that they mean? Do you agree with this idea? Explain.

2. The Constitution requires that presidents be born in the United States. Should it require that Supreme Court justices be native-born too? Why or why not?

Reading Preview

Felix Frankfurter was an immigrant from Austria. He came to the United States when he was 12 years old. He learned English quickly and studied hard. He became a well-known liberal lawyer. He was also an adviser to President Franklin Roosevelt and a Supreme Court justice.

Felix Frankfurter

Felix Frankfurter was a Jewish immigrant from Austria. He came to New York City with his parents when he was a child. Frankfurter learned English quickly. While growing up, he began a lifelong habit. He read several newspapers each day. He attended City College of New York and graduated in 1902. After college, he took some time away from school to earn money. Then he entered Harvard Law School. Frankfurter graduated first in his class in 1906.

After law school, Frankfurter began his long career in law and politics. He became an assistant to Henry Stimpson in the U.S. Attorney's Office in New York. In 1911, Stimpson became Secretary of War for President William Howard Taft. Frankfurter went with him to Washington. There he continued to be Stimpson's assistant.

Frankfurter was known for his clear mind and pleasant manner. In 1914, he began teaching at Harvard Law School. He became a mentor, or adviser, to many of his students. Frankfurter believed that a teacher should share his opinions about the law. So he often invited students to his home to talk. Frankfurter's students said that he pushed them hard. They had to master every point of every case. This hard work gave them a strong background in law. Many of Frankfurter's students later became prominent lawyers.

Frankfurter returned to Washington in 1916, although he also continued to teach. He worked for the Presidential Mediation Committee. This group helped solve labor problems. In 1918, he became chairman of the War Policies Board. In this position, he met Franklin Roosevelt. Roosevelt was then Secretary of the Navy. They began a long friendship. The friendship continued when Roosevelt was governor of New York and when he became president. Frankfurter was a trusted adviser to President Roosevelt.

Frankfurter was a well-known liberal lawyer. He supported defendants in many controversial cases. In 1919 and 1920, some U.S. government officials were worried. They believed that communists were plotting to take over the United States. They arrested thousands of people and held them without trial. Frankfurter and other liberal lawyers were angry. They started the American Civil Liberties Union, or ACLU, in 1920. The ACLU supports people's civil rights.

Frankfurter was also interested in the famous case of Sacco and Vanzetti. In 1920, Sacco and Vanzetti were arrested for armed robbery and murder. They were tried, convicted, and sentenced to death. Many people believed that the trial was unfair. Sacco and Vanzetti were Italian immigrants. They were also anarchists. Anarchists want to get rid of all government. These ideas were unpopular. It is possible the jury convicted them for that reason.

Frankfurter agreed that Sacco and Vanzetti did not get a fair trial. He wrote a long, detailed article about it. He described many problems with the trial. In March 1927, the article appeared in the *Atlantic Monthly*. Frankfurter hoped that publicity from the article would save their lives. But Sacco and Vanzetti died in the electric chair in August 1927.

Franklin Roosevelt became president in 1933. The country was in the middle of the Great Depression. Many people had no work and no money. Roosevelt introduced programs called the New Deal. He made the New Deal programs to help people get through the hard times.

Some Supreme Court justices did not support Roosevelt's new programs. But in 1939 there was an opening on the Supreme Court. Roosevelt nominated Frankfurter to fill it. Supreme Court decisions are not supposed to be based on politics. Even so, presidents usually nominate justices who share their political views. Roosevelt expected Frankfurter to support his programs. The Senate confirmed Frankfurter's nomination unanimously.

Before he became a Supreme Court justice, Frankfurter was known as a liberal. But he stated some unexpected opinions on the court. One controversial opinion came in the case of West Virginia Board of Education vs. Barnette in 1943. In this case, some families in West Virginia refused to let their children salute the U.S. flag in school. They were Jehovah's Witnesses. They said that saluting the flag was against their religion. West Virginia said that all children had to salute the flag.

The case went through the state courts. It finally came to the Supreme Court. The court ruled that West Virginia could not force children to act against their religion. But, in a surprise

"Words are the tools . . . out of which the Constitution was written. Everything depends on an understanding of them."

—Felix Frankfurter[2]

opinion, Frankfurter disagreed. He said that religious groups should not get special treatment. This opinion shocked many of his friends. They expected him to support individual rights in all cases.

Frankfurter was on the Supreme Court until 1962. A stroke forced him to retire then. He always felt proud of being an immigrant who became a Supreme Court justice. His hard work and study had given him that opportunity. Frankfurter died in Washington, D.C., on February 22, 1965.

Comprehension

Complete the sentences. Use information from the reading.

1. As a student, Frankfurter was _____
   _____.

2. While Frankfurter was teaching at Harvard, he _____
   _____.

3. Frankfurter and others started the American Civil Liberties
   Union because _____
   _____.

4. The Sacco and Vanzetti case involved _____
   _____.

5. Frankfurter first met Franklin Roosevelt when _____
   _____.

6. The goal of the New Deal programs was _____
   _____.

7. Presidents usually nominate Supreme Court justices who _____
   _____.

8. On the Supreme Court, Frankfurter surprised people because _____
   _____.

Summary

Check the best summary of the ideas in the reading.

_____ 1. Felix Frankfurter was an immigrant who became a lawyer. He was proud of his immigrant roots.

_____ 2. Felix Frankfurter was an Austrian immigrant, a professor at Harvard Law School, and a Supreme Court justice. He was known as a liberal lawyer. But on the Supreme Court, he stated some surprising opinions.

Vocabulary

Look at these words from the reading. Put a check next to words that you know. Underline words that you don't know yet. Find the words in the reading. Try to guess their meanings.

| anarchist | convict | mentor | prominent |
| controversial | defendant | nominate | unanimously |

Check the correct meaning for each word.

1. mentor

_____ a. student

_____ b. college official

_____ c. adviser or teacher

2. prominent

_____ a. honest

_____ b. well-known

_____ c. smart

3. defendant

_____ a. person accused of a crime

_____ b. person to protect your rights

_____ c. person who helps criminals

4. controversial

_____ a. expected, normal

_____ b. causing disagreement

_____ c. conservative

5. convict

_____ a. to set free

_____ b. to find guilty

_____ c. to arrest

6. anarchist

_____ a. person who opposes all government

_____ b. person who works for the government

_____ c. person who rules others

7. nominate

_____ a. to appoint to a job

_____ b. to talk with

_____ c. to ignore

8. unanimously

_____ a. with a few people disagreeing

_____ b. with someone else deciding

_____ c. with everyone agreeing

Reading a Flow Chart

A flow chart shows the events or actions in a process.

Selecting a New Supreme Court Justice

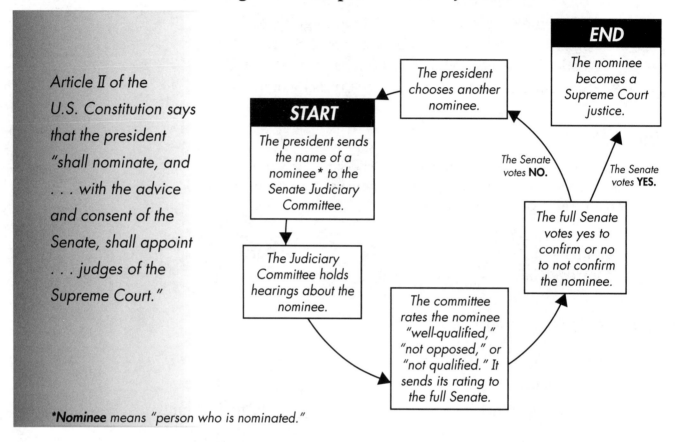

Article II of the U.S. Constitution says that the president "shall nominate, and . . . with the advice and consent of the Senate, shall appoint . . . judges of the Supreme Court."

START
The president sends the name of a nominee* to the Senate Judiciary Committee.

The Judiciary Committee holds hearings about the nominee.

The committee rates the nominee "well-qualified," "not opposed," or "not qualified." It sends its rating to the full Senate.

The president chooses another nominee.

The Senate votes **NO.**

The Senate votes **YES.**

The full Senate votes yes to confirm or no to not confirm the nominee.

END
The nominee becomes a Supreme Court justice.

*__Nominee__ means "person who is nominated."

Complete the sentences. Use information from the flow chart.

1. The rules about appointing Supreme Court justices are in the _____.

2. After the Judiciary Committee gets the name of the president's nominee, it _____

_____.

3. The Judiciary Committee sends its rating to _____

_____.

4. If the Senate does not confirm the president's nominee, _____

_____.

Discuss: Why does the Constitution require the president and Senate to select Supreme Court justices together?

Connecting Today and Yesterday

1. Six Supreme Court justices were immigrants. Do you think that it is important to have justices with immigrant backgrounds on the Supreme Court? Why or why not?

2. The first black Supreme Court justice was Thurgood Marshall. He began his term in 1963. Do you think that it is important to have justices from ethnic minorities on the Supreme Court? Why or why not?

Group Activities

1. In your group, research the five other Supreme Court justices who were immigrants. Who were they? Where did they come from? What are they known for?

2. Research the Pledge of Allegiance. Who wrote it? When did Americans start saying it to salute the flag? Bring a copy of it to class and read it together.

Class Discussion

1. How did Frankfurter achieve so much success? What obstacles did he overcome?

2. What did Frankfurter's students admire about him?

3. Why were Frankfurter's friends surprised by his opinion in the case of West Virginia Board of Education vs. Barnette?

4. Do you think that all schoolchildren should salute the flag and say the Pledge of Allegiance? Do you think that they should have a choice? Explain your opinion.

5. Frankfurter's opinions were sometimes liberal and sometimes conservative. Why? Explain your opinion.

Reflections

1. What was the most interesting thing that you read in this lesson?

2. Can you use anything from Felix Frankfurter's story in your own life? Explain.

3. How can you learn more about Felix Frankfurter or the Supreme Court?

Daniel Webster said, "The law: It has honored us; may we honor it."[3]

How did Frankfurter's life reflect this idea?

Rachel Carson

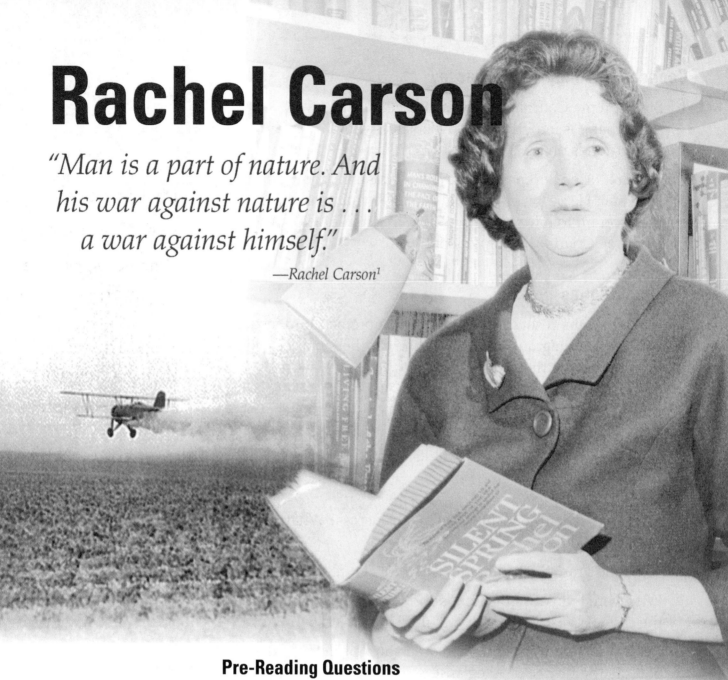

"Man is a part of nature. And his war against nature is . . . a war against himself."

—Rachel Carson[1]

Pre-Reading Questions

1. Read the words below the title. What do you think that they mean? Do you agree or disagree?

2. Do you think that it is good or bad to spray pesticides on food to kill insects? Explain. How do pesticides affect the environment?

Reading Preview

Rachel Carson was a scientist and writer. Her work started the modern environmental movement. Carson's most famous book was *Silent Spring*. This book described the dangers of pesticides. It was the first book to alert the public to risks from these chemicals.

Rachel Carson

Rachel Carson was born on May 27, 1907, on a farm in Springdale, Pennsylvania. From her childhood, she loved both writing and nature. When she was only 10, she published her first article in a children's magazine. In college, Carson was a zoology major. After getting her master's degree, she taught zoology at the University of Maryland. This job let her share her interest in nature. In the summers, she continued her studies at the Marine Biology Lab in Wood's Hole, Massachusetts.

The Marine Biology Lab was located directly on the ocean. Carson became fascinated by the mysteries under the sea. She soon began working part-time for the Federal Bureau of Fisheries. She wrote radio scripts about the sea. In 1936, she applied for a job as a full-time biologist. She was the first woman to pass the civil service test for this job.

While working for the Bureau of Fisheries, Carson wrote about undersea life. Her writing was published in *The New Yorker* magazine. Eventually it became her book *The Sea Around Us.* In this book, Carson described the beauty of the sea. Her words were poetic but easy to understand. The book was popular and won many awards. It earned so much money that Carson retired from her job in 1952. She worked full-time on her writing.

For years, Carson had been concerned about the environment. As early as 1945, she became alarmed about the chemicals that were sprayed over farming areas. Carson knew that these chemicals damaged the environment. But she believed that people did not know about the risks.

Chemical weapons were used in World War I. Later, people realized that the same chemicals could kill weeds, insects, and rodents. Without weeds and pests, farms could produce more crops. Some of the chemicals were released for public use in the 1940s. Pesticides and weed killers became popular. In 1960, more than 637,666,000 pounds of chemical pesticides were produced in the United States.[2]

Carson was particularly concerned about the pesticide DDT. This chemical is stored in plants and in the tissues of animals, including humans. Experiments showed that DDT moves through the food chain. For example, researchers put DDT on grass and then fed the grass to chickens. When these chickens laid eggs, the eggs contained DDT. When animals ate the eggs, their tissues contained DDT. In humans, DDT damages genes, the liver, and the nervous system. Carson learned that people were spraying DDT from airplanes. She decided to write a book about the danger of pesticides and weed killers.

Carson researched her topic from 1958 to 1962. During that time, she had many personal problems. A niece died, and Carson adopted the niece's son. Her mother also died. Carson had cared for her mother for years. And Carson learned that she herself had cancer. However, even with these difficulties, Carson was determined to complete her book.

Carson's book was called *Silent Spring.* It was published in 1962. Chemical makers criticized it. However, the public and many scientists loved it. The book begins with a dramatic story of a possible future. All the birds are dead—killed by unsafe chemicals. People do not hear birds singing in the spring. Instead, the spring is silent.

After its dramatic beginning, *Silent Spring* describes the effects of the chemicals that kill weeds, insects, and rodents. It shows that these chemicals poison lakes, rivers, wildlife, and humans. Carson says that the government should regulate pesticides and weed killers. And she calls for a ban on DDT. She also asks for research to find safer ways to control weeds and pests.

As a result of *Silent Spring,* President John F. Kennedy appointed a committee. The committee investigated Carson's claims. The committee's study agreed with Carson's conclusions. This study led to the start of the federal Environmental Protection Agency. *Silent Spring* also opened up public discussion on pesticides, weed killers, and other chemicals. Many people began to work for a cleaner, safer environment. Volunteer groups began to watch for problems in the environment. It was the start of the environmental movement in the United States.

Because of Carson's work, the government eventually put a ban on DDT. Many businesses had opposed her. But she had courageously told the truth about the dangers of pesticides and other chemicals. Carson died at age 56 in 1964, almost two years after *Silent Spring* was published.

Comprehension

Check the correct answer.

1. From the time Carson was a child, she

   _____ a. wanted to photograph ocean life.

   _____ b. loved nature and writing.

   _____ c. worried about the environment.

2. *The Sea Around Us*

   _____ a. described sea life.

   _____ b. described the dangers of chemicals in the ocean.

   _____ c. was not popular.

3. Carson decided to write about chemicals because

   _____ a. she wanted to be famous.

   _____ b. she needed the money.

   _____ c. she thought that people didn't understand the dangers.

4. Many pesticides that were used in the 1950s

   _____ a. were invented to kill farming pests.

   _____ b. were first used as weapons.

   _____ c. were never released to the public.

5. Carson worried about DDT because it

   _____ a. remains in plants and in animal tissue.

   _____ b. was used in other countries.

   _____ c. kills insects and weeds.

6. Carson wrote *Silent Spring* when

   _____ a. she had lots of free time.

   _____ b. the government asked for it.

   _____ c. she had many problems.

7. In *Silent Spring,* Carson calls for

   _____ a. a ban on all dangerous chemicals.

   _____ b. regulating DDT.

   _____ c. a ban on DDT and regulating other chemicals.

Sequence

Work with a partner. Number the events in the correct order.

_____ Carson teaches zoology at the University of Maryland.

_____ *Silent Spring* is published.

_____ President Kennedy appoints a committee to study chemicals.

_____ Carson writes radio scripts about the sea.

_____ Carson learns that people are spraying DDT from the air.

_____ Carson passes the civil service test to become a full-time biologist.

Vocabulary

Look at these words from the reading. Put a check next to words that you know. Underline words that you don't know yet. Find the words in the reading. Try to guess their meanings.

ban	pesticides	rodents	tissues
food chain	regulate	stored	zoology

Use the words to fill in the blanks in the story.

Rachel Carson began her scientific career as a teacher of _____ .
                                                                                    1

Then she studied and wrote about the ocean. She later became

concerned about _____ . These chemicals were used to kill insects,
                                            2

_____ , and other farming pests. Carson was most concerned about the
            3

chemical DDT, which was _____ in plants and in animal
                                                    4

_____ . Therefore it could move through the _____ .
            5   6

She wanted the government to _____ all pesticides and to put a
                                                    7

_____ on DDT.
            8

Reading a Chart

A chart is a useful way to organize facts.

Some Actions to Protect the Environment

Action	Year	What it is	What it does	Why
Lead-Based Paint Poisoning Prevention Act	1971	U.S. federal law	forbids using lead-based paint • in housing built or repaired with federal money • on dishes, toys, or furniture	to prevent lead poisoning
Ban on DDT	1972	EPA regulation	forbids most uses of DDT in the U.S.	to prevent environmental damage by DDT
Safe Drinking Water Act	1974	U.S. federal law	sets health standards for public drinking water	to protect people from unsafe drinking water
Montreal Protocol	1987	treaty signed by the U.S. and 23 other nations	controls the use of chemicals called CFCs (Later, the 24 nations agreed to a ban on CFCs.)	to protect the earth's ozone layer (CFCs damage the ozone layer.)
Federal Agency Recycling Policy	1991	order by the U.S. president	requires U.S. federal agencies to • recycle their trash • use recycled products	to reduce pollution and save natural resources

Answer the questions. Use information from the chart.

1. When did the United States put a ban on DDT? _____

2. Which action helps create a safer supply of drinking water? _____

    _____

3. Which action helps save wood and paper? _____

4. What is the Montreal Protocol? _____

    _____

5. Which action protects people from lead poisoning? _____

    _____

Discuss: Which of these actions do you think is most important? Why?

Carson believed that people who think about the beauty of the earth will never feel alone or tired of life.

How was this true in Carson's life?

Connecting Today and Yesterday

1. Should pesticides still be regulated? Should they be used at all? Explain your opinion.

2. Organic farming uses methods such as friendly insects and plants that help keep pests away. But sometimes these methods don't work as well as chemicals. Do you think that all U.S. farms should become organic? Why or why not?

Group Activity

Get *Silent Spring* from the library. Read the introduction. Then discuss these questions in your group.

1. Why did Carson use this story to begin the book?

2. Do you think that the story could come true? Why or why not?

Class Discussion

1. Why did Americans use so many pesticides and weed killers in the 1940s and 1950s?

2. Why did the companies that made chemicals criticize *Silent Spring?*

3. Why was Carson worried about DDT?

4. Carson wrote *Silent Spring* at a difficult time in her life. Why was she so motivated? Explain your opinion.

5. How was the U.S. Environmental Protection Agency founded?

Reflections

1. What was the most interesting thing that you read in this lesson?

2. Can you use anything from Rachel Carson's story in your own life? Explain.

3. How can you learn more about Rachel Carson or the environmental movement?

César Chávez

"¡Sí, Se Puede!"
(Spanish: "Yes, it can be done!")

—*slogan of the United Farm Workers*

Pre-Reading Questions

1. Read the words below the title. When do you think that a leader might use these words?

2. What are the working conditions for farm workers? Name some things that farm workers need to be concerned about.

Reading Preview

César Chávez was a labor organizer. He brought national attention to working conditions for farm workers in the United States. These conditions were difficult and sometimes dangerous. Chávez successfully led the first national farm workers' union. His commitment to workers' rights added spirit to the growing Chicano movement.

César Chávez

César Chávez was born in 1927 near Yuma, Arizona. As a child, he heard his grandfather's stories about the Mexican Revolution. He also heard about problems between the rich and the poor. Chávez saw his mother feed hungry people who came to their door. Before bed, his mother told the children *cuentos*, or stories. These stories contained moral lessons. His grandmother taught him about religion. He went to mass with her every week. Chávez's life was shaped by his family's spirituality and commitment to the poor.

In the 1930s, Chávez's family suffered in the Great Depression. They lost their farm in Yuma. The entire family became migrant workers. They traveled through Arizona and California looking for farm work. Chávez saw that farm workers faced injustices every day. Growers often paid very low wages and made workers pay high rents for housing.

When Chávez was in eighth grade, his father was injured and couldn't work anymore. Chávez became a full-time farm worker.

Chávez spent two years in the Navy and then returned to California. He married Helen Fabela. He had known her since he was 15 years old. They moved to San José, where Chávez worked as a laborer. Chávez also became involved with the Community Service Organization. This group fought discrimination against Mexican Americans. It supported workers in labor disputes. At the Community Service Organization, Chávez learned about labor relations. He also learned about the beliefs and leadership style of Mahatma Gandhi in India. Later, Chávez used Gandhi's strategy of fasting to bring attention to his cause.

Chávez wanted the Community Service Organization to organize farm workers. When the group refused, Chávez quit. He decided to build a labor union for farm workers. Chávez moved his family to Delano, California. He went from farm to farm, talking to the workers. He told them about a new union called the United Farm Workers, or UFW. He explained why they needed labor contracts.

Chávez opened his home to farm workers who needed help. He became famous for his optimism and persistence. Soon, more than 1,000 workers had joined the UFW. The union's slogan was

"¡Sí, Se Puede!" It means "Yes, it can be done!" It says that the union can overcome any obstacle.

In 1965, Chávez gained national attention and sympathy for the farm workers. There was a conflict between the laborers who picked grapes and the large wine makers that owned the farms. The companies often brought in workers just for the grape harvest. On some farms, these "imported" workers got higher wages than the workers who worked there every day.

Chávez and the UFW decided to protest these unfair wages. They wanted permanent contracts for the grape pickers. The union voted to go on strike against the grape growers in the Delano area of California. Chávez called for Americans to boycott grapes and wine, and people stopped buying them. The national media showed the strikers on picket lines.

In the 1960s, many people were working to make the United States a fairer society. Other workers traveled to California to help the strikers. Chávez's struggle became part of a social and political trend of the time.

The grape strike lasted five years. Sometimes strikers faced violence. But the UFW had a commitment to nonviolence. In February 1968, Chávez began fasting. On the 25th day, he ended his fasting in a county park. Thousands of union supporters held a Catholic mass there. Senator Robert Kennedy spoke emotionally about Chávez and the farm workers.

In 1970, Chávez and the UFW saw results. The public was putting pressure on the growers. Many growers wanted to settle the dispute. They signed contracts with almost 85 percent of the grape pickers. These contracts provided better working conditions. At that time, the Chicano, or Mexican American, movement was growing. Publicity for the farm workers gave momentum to that movement too.

The 1980s, however, were more conservative. The UFW lost many labor disputes. Yet Chávez worked tirelessly. He gained more contracts for grape pickers. He also helped lettuce and vegetable workers get contracts and better working conditions.

In the early 1990s, the UFW had financial and legal problems. Growers who lost money during the grape strike sued the union.

"A symbol is an important thing. That is why we chose an Aztec eagle. It gives pride. . . . When people see it, they know it means dignity."

—César Chávez[1]

On April 23, 1993, Chávez was in Arizona. He was going to testify there in a lawsuit. He had just finished fasting. He was exhausted when he went to sleep. The next day the world was shocked to learn that Chávez had died in his sleep.

Chávez is remembered for his courage and for his belief in the value of every human being. In 1994, President Bill Clinton recognized Chávez with a major posthumous award. It was the Presidential Medal of Freedom, the highest civilian honor in the United States.

Comprehension

Complete the sentences. Use information from the reading.

1. Chávez became a full-time farm worker when _____
   _____.

2. The Community Service Organization worked to _____
   _____.

3. Chávez quit the Community Service Organization because _____
   _____.

4. To find members for the new UFW, Chávez _____
   _____.

5. In 1965, grape pickers went on strike because _____
   _____.

6. In the 1960s, people stopped buying grapes and wine because _____
   _____.

7. Chávez fasted in 1968 because _____
   _____.

8. The UFW had problems in the 1990s because _____
   _____.

Sequence

Work with a partner. Number the events in the correct order.

_____ The United Farm Workers is founded.

_____ Chávez works at the Community Service Organization.

_____ Grape pickers go on strike.

_____ Chávez fasts for 25 days.

_____ Chávez plans to testify in an Arizona lawsuit.

Vocabulary

Look at these words from the reading. Put a check next to words that you know. Underline words that you don't know yet. Find the words in the reading. Try to guess their meanings.

boycott	dispute	migrant	posthumous
commitment	fast	momentum	strike

Check the correct meaning for each word.

1. commitment
   _____ a. belief
   _____ b. happiness
   _____ c. suspicion

2. migrant
   _____ a. hard-working
   _____ b. traveling around
   _____ c. living in one place

3. dispute
   _____ a. disagreement
   _____ b. meeting
   _____ c. silence

4. fast
   _____ a. to refuse to speak
   _____ b. to refuse to sleep
   _____ c. to refuse to eat

5. strike
   _____ a. refusing to buy
   _____ b. refusing to work
   _____ c. refusing to talk

6. boycott
   _____ a. to refuse to buy
   _____ b. to refuse to work
   _____ c. to refuse to talk to

7. momentum
   _____ a. energy
   _____ b. money
   _____ c. supplies

8. posthumous
   _____ a. unfair
   _____ b. late
   _____ c. given after death

Reading a Time Line

A time line shows dates and events in order on a line.

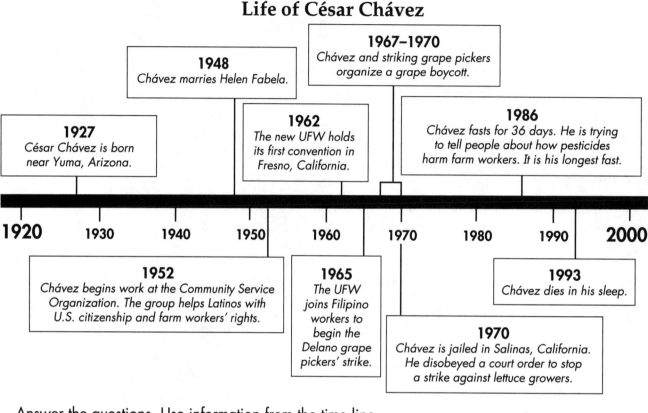

Life of César Chávez

Answer the questions. Use information from the time line.

1. In what year did Chávez join the Community Service
   Organization? _____

2. How did the Community Service Organization help
   Mexican Americans? _____

   _____

3. In what years did farm workers try to get people to support their
   strike by boycotting grapes? _____

4. In what year did Chávez fast for the longest time? _____

5. What was the reason that he fasted then? _____

   _____

6. In what year was Chávez jailed in Salinas, California? _____

7. Chávez led the UFW from its beginning until he died. For how
   many years did he lead the union? _____

Connecting Today and Yesterday

1. What issues did farm workers face in the 1960s? What issues do they face today?

2. March 31, César Chávez's birthday, is César Chávez Day in many parts of the United States. Why is there a holiday in his honor? Do you know how this holiday is celebrated?

Group Activities

1. Research the UFW strike that began in 1965. How did TV and newspapers report the story? Look for interviews with Chávez. Then tell your group about what Chávez said.

2. Bring in a picture of the UFW flag. Why was it an important symbol for Chávez and his union? Discuss in your group.

Class Discussion

1. How did early experiences influence Chávez's attitudes and beliefs?

2. Why did Chávez's family become migrant farm workers?

3. What did Chávez do to get support for the UFW?

4. How did TV influence people's attitudes about the UFW strike in 1965? Was the TV coverage a benefit or a disadvantage for the farm workers?

5. What are Chávez's most important contributions to U.S. society? Explain your opinion.

Reflections

1. What was the most interesting thing that you read in this lesson?

2. Can you use anything from César Chávez's story in your own life? Explain.

3. How can you learn more about César Chávez or the UFW?

Robert Kennedy called César Chávez "one of the heroic figures of our time."[2]

Why did he say that? Do you agree? Why or why not?

Rosa Parks

"I just wanted to be free like everybody else."

—*Rosa Parks*[1]

Pre-Reading Questions

1. Did you ever hear of Rosa Parks? What do you know about her? Look at the words below the title. Why did she say this?

2. Would you ever think about disobeying a law? Explain.

Reading Preview

Rosa Parks grew up in a society that discriminated against black people. All her life, she wanted blacks and whites to be treated equally. Then one day in 1955, this quiet, courageous woman did something that changed U.S. history. With a simple action, she became a symbol of the fight for equal rights.

Rosa Parks

When Rosa Parks was growing up in the south, blacks and whites were segregated in public places. Blacks and whites had separate schools, separate waiting rooms for trains and buses, and separate sections in restaurants. On buses, blacks had to sit in the back. If a white person needed a seat, black passengers had to stand up.

Rosa McCauley was born on February 4, 1913, in Tuskegee, Alabama. Her father was a carpenter and builder, and her mother was a schoolteacher. Rosa's mother encouraged her to study and work hard for success. When Rosa was very young, her parents separated, and her mother took Rosa to live with her grandparents. They moved to a small, quiet town called Pine Valley, Alabama. Rosa spent her elementary school years there.

In 1898, the Supreme Court had ruled that "separate but equal" facilities for black and white people were legal. As a result, many southern states had separate facilities for blacks and whites. But often the facilities were not equal. Facilities for blacks were usually inferior to the ones for whites. And laws discriminated against blacks who wanted to vote. Blacks had trouble getting good jobs. White racist groups, such as the Ku Klux Klan, used violence to intimidate blacks. They wanted blacks to be afraid of moving up in society.

As a child, Rosa saw the problems of racial segregation. Her mother taught at an all-black school. Rosa herself went to a one-room schoolhouse for blacks. It had no desks and no heat. She also saw her grandfather sleep with a rifle so that he could protect his family. She later said, "I remember . . . hearing the Klan ride at night and hearing a lynching [a murder by hanging]."[2] She was afraid that the house would burn down.

In 1924, Rosa and her mother moved to Montgomery, Alabama. There, she continued her education. In 1931, she met Raymond Parks, a local barber. He was active in the civil rights movement. Rosa McCauley and Raymond Parks married in 1932. At that time, she worked as a seamstress. She also volunteered as the secretary of the local chapter of the National Association for the Advancement of Colored People, or NAACP.

On December 1, 1955, Rosa Parks was going home from work. She got on the bus and sat down. After a few stops, the bus filled up. A white man wanted her seat. The bus driver ordered Parks to stand up. Parks remembers thinking about how unfair it was to make her move. She said no and sat still. The bus driver called the police. A policeman got onto the bus and asked Parks why she didn't get up. Parks answered, "I don't think I should have to. Why do you push us around so?" The police took her to jail. Civil rights leader E. D. Nixon, who was Parks's friend, paid her bail, so she was able to go home later that night.

Blacks were angry about Parks's arrest. The NAACP wanted to fight segregation on the buses. A group of civil rights leaders in Montgomery, including Martin Luther King, Jr., organized blacks to boycott Montgomery buses. More than 90 percent of black passengers stayed off the buses. Blacks who had cars drove people who needed rides. Other people walked miles to work. Most of the buses were almost empty for over a year.

Boycotting the buses and Parks's courageous refusal to give up her seat received publicity throughout the country. Black groups in Montgomery took the dispute to federal court. In February 1956, they sued to stop bus segregation. They won, but the city appealed to the Supreme Court. Finally, on November 13, 1956, the Supreme Court ruled that segregation on buses was unconstitutional.

Over the next 10 years, many blacks and whites worked to improve civil rights for blacks and other minorities. There were also important changes in U.S. federal laws. "Separate but equal" facilities were now illegal. The Civil Rights Act became law in 1964. It outlawed discriminating against minorities in housing and employment. The Voting Rights Act of 1965 soon followed. It outlawed using fees, literacy tests, and other methods to stop blacks from voting.

Parks's courageous act had helped the progress of civil rights. But she still had a dream. She wanted to help young people. With Elaine Eason Steele, she started the Rosa and Raymond Parks Institute for Self-Development in 1987. This organization teaches young people about their history. It also helps them build the skills that they need to achieve their dreams.

Comprehension

Check the correct answer.

1. When Rosa Parks was growing up,

    _____ a. blacks and whites were segregated.

    _____ b. blacks and whites had equal rights.

    _____ c. blacks were slaves.

2. In 1898, the Supreme Court ruled that

    _____ a. segregation was illegal.

    _____ b. segregation was legal if the facilities were equal.

    _____ c. whites were superior.

3. In places that had separate facilities for blacks and whites,

    _____ a. the facilities were usually equal.

    _____ b. the facilities for whites were usually better.

    _____ c. the facilities for blacks were usually better.

4. People in the civil rights movement believed that

    _____ a. no action should be taken to fight segregation.

    _____ b. all people should be treated equally.

    _____ c. blacks and whites were not equal.

5. When civil rights leaders heard that Parks was arrested,

    _____ a. they organized blacks to boycott Montgomery buses.

    _____ b. they called the mayor.

    _____ c. they wrote Parks a letter.

6. In the 1960s, new federal laws

    _____ a. outlawed only fees for voting.

    _____ b. outlawed only segregated housing.

    _____ c. outlawed fees for voting, segregated housing, and other ways of discriminating against blacks.

7. The Rosa and Raymond Parks Institute

    _____ a. hasn't been started yet.

    _____ b. finds jobs for young people.

    _____ c. helps young people learn history and skills.

Sequence

Work with a partner. Number the events in the correct order.

_____ Rosa McCauley moves to Montgomery, Alabama.

_____ The Rosa and Raymond Parks Institute is founded.

_____ The Supreme Court says that segregated buses are unconstitutional.

_____ Rosa McCauley lives in Pine Valley, Alabama.

_____ Black passengers begin boycotting Montgomery buses.

_____ Parks refuses to give up her seat.

Vocabulary

Look at these words from the reading. Put a check next to words that you know. Underline words that you don't know yet. Find the words in the reading. Try to guess their meanings.

courageous	facilities	lynchings	segregation
discriminated	intimidate	racist	unconstitutional

Use the words to fill in the blanks in the story.

Rosa Parks grew up in a society that _____ against black people. At
1

that time, racial _____ kept blacks and whites apart. Separate public
2

and educational _____, such as schools or restaurants, were legal. The
3

Ku Klux Klan and other _____ groups used _____
4 5

and other violence to _____ blacks. Then in 1955, Parks took a
6

_____ action. She refused to give up her seat on a bus and was arrested.
7

To protest Parks's arrest, blacks in Montgomery, Alabama, decided

to boycott the buses. Finally, the Supreme Court declared that

segregated buses were _____.
8

Reading a Time Line

A time line shows dates and events in order on a line.

Events in the History of U.S. Civil Rights Laws

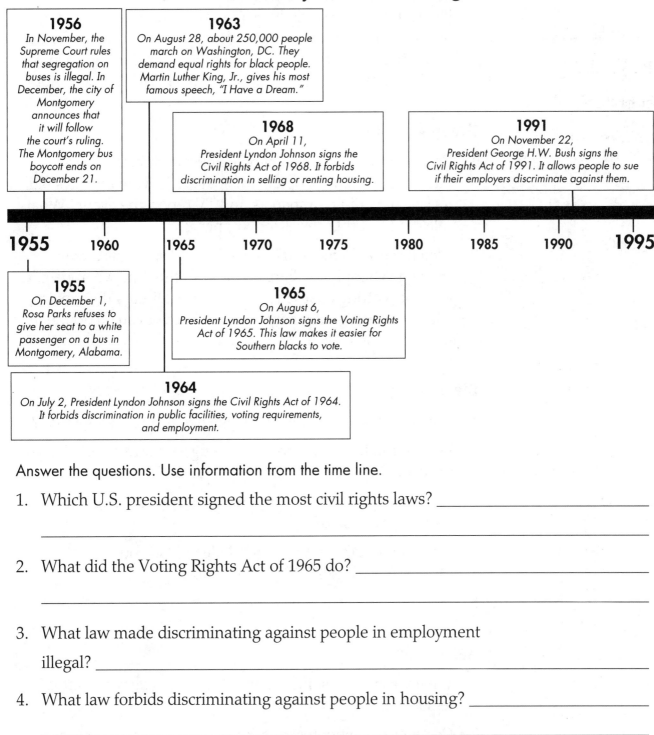

1956
In November, the Supreme Court rules that segregation on buses is illegal. In December, the city of Montgomery announces that it will follow the court's ruling. The Montgomery bus boycott ends on December 21.

1963
On August 28, about 250,000 people march on Washington, DC. They demand equal rights for black people. Martin Luther King, Jr., gives his most famous speech, "I Have a Dream."

1968
On April 11, President Lyndon Johnson signs the Civil Rights Act of 1968. It forbids discrimination in selling or renting housing.

1991
On November 22, President George H.W. Bush signs the Civil Rights Act of 1991. It allows people to sue if their employers discriminate against them.

1955   1960   1965   1970   1975   1980   1985   1990   1995

1955
On December 1, Rosa Parks refuses to give her seat to a white passenger on a bus in Montgomery, Alabama.

1965
On August 6, President Lyndon Johnson signs the Voting Rights Act of 1965. This law makes it easier for Southern blacks to vote.

1964
On July 2, President Lyndon Johnson signs the Civil Rights Act of 1964. It forbids discrimination in public facilities, voting requirements, and employment.

Answer the questions. Use information from the time line.

1. Which U.S. president signed the most civil rights laws? _____

    _____

2. What did the Voting Rights Act of 1965 do? _____

    _____

3. What law made discriminating against people in employment

    illegal? _____

4. What law forbids discriminating against people in housing? _____

    _____

Discuss: Do you think that it is fair to let workers sue if their employer discriminates against them? Why or why not?

Many people call Rosa Parks "the Mother of the Civil Rights Movement."

Do you agree? Why or why not?

Connecting Today and Yesterday

1. Did someone ever discriminate against someone you know because of skin color or ethnicity? Describe what happened.

2. In the United States, discriminating against minorities is illegal. But police sometimes use "racial profiling." They decide that certain ethnic groups may be involved in a crime. Then they question people from those ethnic groups. Do you think that racial profiling should be legal? Why or why not?

Group Activities

1. Research the time when people boycotted the Montgomery buses. How many people participated? How many days did it last? How did newspapers and TV report the event? What role did Martin Luther King, Jr., play?

2. Watch the 1991 movie *The Long Walk Home.* This movie, starring Whoopi Goldberg, deals with the time when people were boycotting buses in Montgomery. Discuss the movie. Did anything about it surprise you? Would you recommend it to other people? Why or why not?

Class Discussion

1. Why did Rosa Parks refuse to give her seat to a white man?

2. Do you think that the police were right to arrest Parks? If you were a police officer, what would you do? Why?

3. Why were people in the civil rights movement angry that Parks was arrested?

4. Do you think that it was a good idea to boycott the Montgomery buses? Why or why not?

5. How did Parks change U.S. history?

Reflections

1. What was the most interesting thing that you read in this lesson?

2. Can you use anything from Rosa Parks's story in your own life? Explain.

3. How can you learn more about Rosa Parks or the civil rights movement?

Billy Frank, Jr.

"I speak for the salmon, and try to build bridges of understanding between Indian and non-Indian people."

—*Billy Frank, Jr.*[1]

Pre-Reading Questions

1. Look at the words below the title. What do you think that they mean? Explain.

2. The salmon is an important symbol in Native American culture in the Pacific Northwest. Why?

Reading Preview

Billy Frank, Jr., is a Native American from the Nisqually tribe in the Pacific Northwest. He has worked for many years to solve conflicts over Native American fishing rights. He has fought for rights that the U.S. government guaranteed long ago. His courageous actions have helped Native Americans and have also helped protect the environment.

Billy Frank, Jr.

Billy Frank, Jr., was born in 1931 on the Nisqually reservation, along the Nisqually River in the state of Washington. His father, Billy Frank, was the last full-blooded Nisqually Indian. As young Frank grew up, he learned to be proud of his heritage. His father taught him the customs and beliefs of their people.

Frank often went salmon fishing with his father. They fished at Frank's Landing. This place on the Nisqually River was named for their family. Frank's father once said that if there were no more salmon, there would be no more Indians. That comment made an impression on Frank. He devoted his life to the survival of the salmon and the Nisqually.

Many Nisqually stories describe a sacred connection between salmon and Native people. The Nisqually were allowed to follow their traditions until the mid-1800s. At that time, the U.S. government offered free land in the Pacific Northwest to white Americans. White settlers came to live on Native land. Conflicts arose between these settlers and Native people.

To solve the conflicts, the U.S. government made treaties with the tribal leaders. The Native Americans gave up much of their land. But the government guaranteed that they would have unrestricted fishing rights. These rights let them fish freely on their reservations and in other traditional places.

Over time, a large commercial fishing industry began. Whites opened fish canneries and dammed the rivers for electricity. As a result, the number of salmon decreased sharply. So the Washington state government set up new agencies. These agencies issued fishing licenses to control how many salmon people could catch. They also set up restricted areas. No fishing was allowed in those areas.

Native people, however, claimed that they had the right to fish anywhere without licenses. They said that the treaties guaranteed those rights. There were many court cases over this issue. Sometimes courts ruled in favor of the state government. Sometimes they ruled in favor of the Native Americans.

Frank was introduced to this conflict in 1945, when he was 14. According to state authorities, Native people needed licenses to fish at Frank's Landing. Frank's father believed that the treaties guaranteed his family the right to fish there. One day, Frank's father took him to fish at Frank's Landing. They knew that fishing there was against state law. They knew that they might be arrested, and state authorities did arrest them.

When Frank grew up, he decided to continue his father's fight for fishing rights. He organized groups of Native people to protest the fishing regulations. They protested by fishing in restricted areas without licenses. From the 1950s to the 1970s, Frank was arrested and jailed more than 40 times. At times, the protests led to violence between Native people and state officials. During one protest in 1964, Frank suffered a terrible personal loss. State authorities seized his traditional family canoe. The canoe was a precious part of Frank's heritage. But he was determined to continue the fight for Native rights.

In the 1970s, the federal government ordered the Justice Department to review Native American complaints. District Judge George Boldt carefully studied the treaties between Native Americans and the U.S. government. Then he interpreted the language of the treaties. He ruled that the state could not restrict Indian fishing. According to Boldt, the treaties meant that Indians and whites should share the fish from the Indians' traditional fishing places. Therefore, Boldt said, Native fishermen should get half of the catch. He said that they could control their own fishing.

Native people were happy with this decision. But Frank worried about the future relationship between Native people and Washington state. He knew that both sides had to cooperate and put aside bad feelings. This was the only way to keep the environment clean, with lots of fish. Frank worked to bring both sides together. He organized the Northwest Indian Fisheries Commission. Twenty tribal groups in Washington state made up this organization. They worked with the state government on environmental issues.

Frank also negotiated with the state government and the timber industry. He helped reform logging and pesticide use. These reforms helped increase the population of bald eagles in the Northwest, among other benefits.

In 1980, Frank got a surprise from state officials. They found Frank's family canoe in a warehouse and returned it to him. The

"We were always ready to . . . go back to jail."

—*Billy Frank, Jr.*[2]

wood was rotted, so the boat could not be used on the water. But Frank made it the symbol of the new cooperative relationship between Native people and the state government.

In 1992, Frank received the prestigious Albert Schweitzer Humanitarian Award. This award honored Frank for peace-making and working to improve the environment. Other groups have learned from him. They have used his method of peaceful negotiation to solve environmental conflicts.

Comprehension

Complete the sentences. Use information from the reading.

1. Billy Frank, Jr., was proud of his Native American heritage

   because _____

   _____.

2. Salmon were important to the Nisqually because _____

   _____.

3. When commercial fishing began in Washington state, _____

   _____.

4. Frank was arrested and jailed many times because _____

   _____.

5. Judge Boldt decided that _____

   _____.

6. Frank organized the Northwest Indian Fisheries Commission

   because _____

   _____.

7. When Frank got back his canoe, _____

   _____.

Summary

Check the best summary of the ideas in the reading.

_____ 1. Billy Frank, Jr., is a Nisqually Native American who protested unfair fishing laws. He went to jail many times.

_____ 2. Billy Frank, Jr., is a Nisqually Native American who fought for fair fishing rights. He helped expand cooperation between the government and Native Americans.

Vocabulary

Look at these words from the reading. Put a check next to words that you know. Underline words that you don't know yet. Find the words in the reading. Try to guess their meanings.

authorities	heritage	prestigious	seize
determined	interpret	sacred	unrestricted

Check the correct meaning for each word.

1. heritage
   - _____ a. traditions
   - _____ b. tools
   - _____ c. handcrafts

2. sacred
   - _____ a. unimportant
   - _____ b. holy
   - _____ c. emotional

3. unrestricted
   - _____ a. with no limits
   - _____ b. limited
   - _____ c. legal

4. authorities
   - _____ a. laws
   - _____ b. citizens
   - _____ c. government officials

5. seize
   - _____ a. to destroy
   - _____ b. to take away
   - _____ c. to inspect

6. determined
   - _____ a. committed
   - _____ b. angry
   - _____ c. afraid

7. interpret
   - _____ a. to explain
   - _____ b. to cancel
   - _____ c. to ignore

8. prestigious
   - _____ a. expensive
   - _____ b. showing great honor
   - _____ c. unimportant

Reading a Map

Physical maps show features of land and water. **Political maps** show borders between countries, states, or other organized territories. Many maps, like this one, combine both types. It shows physical features of the Pacific Northwest. It also shows Native American lands and other political features.

Native American Land in the Pacific Northwest

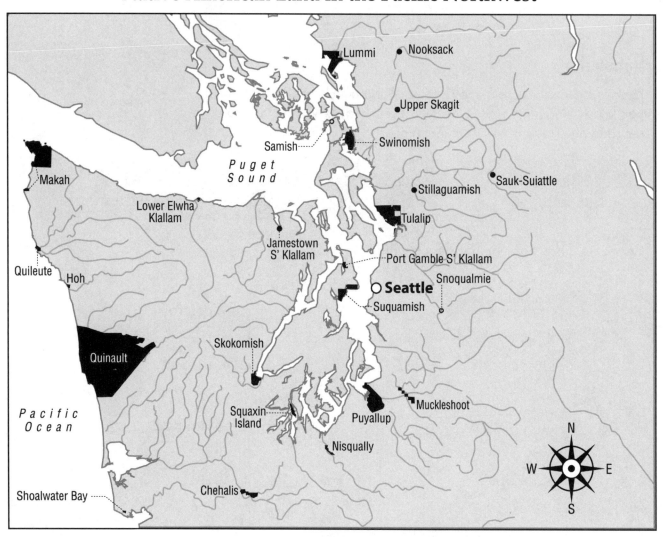

Answer the questions. Use information from the map.

1. How many Native American lands are in the Pacific Northwest? _____

2. What direction is Seattle from the Nisqually tribe? _____

3. Which tribe is farthest to the northwest? _____

4. What natural resource borders most of the tribal locations? _____

Connecting Today and Yesterday

1. In the past, many Americans thought that Native Americans should speak only English and forget their traditional culture. Do you think that this attitude has changed today? Explain.

2. Native Americans could not be U.S. citizens until Congress passed the Citizen Act in 1924. Why did it take so long for Native Americans to become citizens?

Group Activity

Find books or articles that tell traditional stories from Native American tribes of the Pacific Northwest, such as the Nisqually. Look for stories about salmon and about cultural beliefs. Bring in the stories and articles, and share them with your group. Then discuss the information that is most interesting or surprising to you.

Class Discussion

1. Frank's father knew that they could be arrested for fishing without a license. Why did he take his son fishing anyway? Would you do the same thing? Why or why not?

2. What was the main conflict between the Washington state government and Native Americans over fishing rights?

3. How did Frank protest state fishing regulations? Do you think that his approach was good?

4. Why was Frank's family canoe important to him? Do you know of any other objects that are symbols of cooperation or friendship?

Reflections

1. What was the most interesting thing that you read in this lesson?

2. Can you use anything from Billy Frank, Jr.'s, story in your own life? Explain.

3. How can you learn more about Billy Frank, Jr., or Native American culture in the Pacific Northwest?

"In making any law, our chiefs must always consider three things: the effect of their decision on peace; the effect on the natural world; and the effect on seven generations in the future."

—Carol Jacobs, a Cayuga clan mother[3]

How did Billy Frank, Jr., demonstrate this Native American idea?

Maya Lin

"You touch a name and the pain comes out."

—*Maya Lin, about the Vietnam Veterans Memorial*[1]

Pre-Reading Questions

1. Read the words below the title. What kind of pain is Lin talking about? Explain.

2. How can a country honor its war veterans? What kinds of memorials are appropriate?

Reading Preview

When she was only 21 years old, Maya Lin won an architecture contest. She created a design for the Vietnam Veterans Memorial in Washington, D.C. Her simple design has two stone walls that list the names of dead and missing Americans from the Vietnam War. It has become the most visited memorial in the United States.

Maya Lin

Maya Lin is the daughter of Chinese immigrants. Her parents left China in the 1940s. Lin was born in Athens, Ohio, in 1959. Her mother was a poet. She also taught English and Asian literature. Her father was a well-known ceramic artist. He also directed the fine arts program at Ohio University. Lin's parents didn't talk about their past in China. They didn't teach Lin and her brother the Chinese language. Lin said that she felt more American than Chinese while she was growing up. However, her artwork shows a strong Asian influence. She often uses simple forms in a natural landscape.

As a child, Lin was surrounded by artwork and furniture that her father made. She often made pottery in her father's studio at the university. She also liked to read and to explore nature. Until the eighth grade, Lin attended a progressive private school. Her teachers encouraged her to be an independent thinker. In high school, she was interested in modern European literature. At the same time, she became interested in death.

After high school, Lin enrolled at Yale University. She took many trips to the local cemetery and photographed headstones. She admired the serenity of the simple designs. In her junior year, she studied in Europe. In Copenhagen, Denmark, she visited a cemetery that was also used as a park in the summer. Lin saw that the cemetery was an important part of everyday life. This use of the cemetery fascinated her.

When she returned to Yale, she enrolled in a funerary architecture class—a class that studied memorials for the dead. As a class assignment, the professor asked the students to enter a nationwide competition to design the Vietnam Veterans Memorial. The students all went to Washington, D.C. They visited the location of the future memorial. It was between the Lincoln Memorial and the Capitol building. Lin saw a few people playing catch on the grass there. They reminded her of the cemetery-park in Copenhagen. She got the idea to build a "gravestone in a park."[2]

Lin submitted an innovative design for the competition. She designed two large, black, granite walls that formed a V shape. On the walls would be carved the name of every American who had died or was missing in the Vietnam War. Almost 58,000 names would be cut into the stone. Visitors could touch and photograph the names. Lin hoped that this experience would comfort people who had lost loved ones in the war. Lin won the competition. She was only 21 years old.

When her design became public, its quiet beauty impressed many people. However, some veterans' groups thought that the design did not honor the dead and missing soldiers enough. They thought that it did not look patriotic. The groups wanted a statue of a soldier instead. And some people made racist remarks because of Lin's Asian background.

Lin was under a lot of pressure to change her design. But she kept her original plan. As a compromise, the government allowed the groups who opposed Lin's design to put up a statue. The statue shows three servicemen with a U.S. flag. It stands near the entrance to the memorial. The Vietnam Veterans Memorial, built using Lin's design, opened on November 13, 1982. It is now the most visited memorial in the United States.

After the Vietnam Veterans Memorial opened, Lin enrolled in graduate school at Yale. But she was still upset about the controversy. She couldn't concentrate on her studies. So she worked for an architectural company in Boston for a while. Then she returned to school and graduated in 1986.

As her next public project, Lin designed the Civil Rights Memorial in Montgomery, Alabama. This memorial honored people who died in the fight for racial equality. Lin thought about Dr. Martin Luther King, Jr.,'s speech "I Have a Dream." She remembered the image of water in the speech. King said the fight for equal rights would not end "until justice rolls down like waters."[3]

Lin used that image in her design. The names of the people who died in the civil rights movement are carved on a stone table. The table also lists important events in the movement. Water flows gently over the names and events. The Civil Rights Memorial was dedicated and opened to the public in 1989.

Lin continues to make unique sculptures and architectural designs. She works for museums and private individuals. She has won many awards and honors for her work. She often uses natural images and materials. They show her concern for the environment and the need to protect it.

Comprehension

Check the correct answer.

1. As a child, Lin

   _____ a. showed no interest in art or books.

   _____ b. spent a lot of time playing sports with friends.

   _____ c. spent time alone making pottery or reading.

2. Lin took a funerary architecture class because

   _____ a. she was interested in cemeteries and headstone designs.

   _____ b. she thought that it might improve her photographs of cemeteries.

   _____ c. she felt that it was important to prepare for death.

3. Lin's design for the Vietnam Veterans Memorial included

   _____ a. water running over a table.

   _____ b. a statue of three soldiers.

   _____ c. two black granite walls.

4. When they saw Lin's design, some veterans' groups said

   _____ a. that they needed another wall for all the names.

   _____ b. that it was not patriotic enough.

   _____ c. that the names of missing soldiers should not be listed.

5. When Lin began to design the Civil Rights Memorial,

   _____ a. she worried about having problems with racism.

   _____ b. she remembered Martin Luther King Jr.,'s words about justice.

   _____ c. she planned to use the same design as the Vietnam Veterans Memorial.

6. Lin's most recent work

   _____ a. is only for museums.

   _____ b. includes only memorials for the dead.

   _____ c. includes a focus on the environment.

Sequence

Work with a partner. Number the events in the correct order.

_____ Lin visits Copenhagen.

_____ Lin creates works about the need to protect the environment.

_____ Lin works in her father's studio.

_____ Lin designs the Civil Rights Memorial.

_____ Lin starts at Yale University.

_____ The Vietnam Veterans Memorial opens.

Vocabulary

Look at these words from the reading. Put a check next to words that you know. Underline words that you don't know yet. Find the words in the reading. Try to guess their meanings.

competition	environment	innovative	serenity
compromise	headstones	racial equality	veterans

Use the words to fill in the blanks in the story.

Maya Lin grew up with a strong interest in art. In college, she often

visited the local cemetery. She was impressed by the feeling of _____
1

and the designs on the _____. In her last year of college, she entered
2

and won a _____ to design the Vietnam Veterans Memorial. Her design
3

was _____, with a simple beauty. But it also started a dispute. Some
4

groups of _____ complained that it was not patriotic enough. Lin kept
5

her original plan. But as a _____, the government added a statue of
6

three soldiers nearby. Lin also designed the Civil Rights Memorial.

It honors the people who fought for _____. Some of her most recent
7

work expresses her concern for the natural _____.
8

Reading a Map

Road maps show roads, highways, and other travel information. This map shows part of the National Mall in Washington, D.C. The mall is a favorite place for tourists. It has many of the most famous monuments in the United States.

Western End of the National Mall

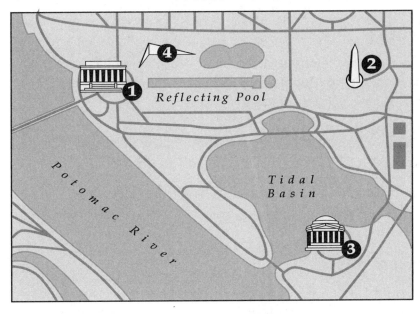

1 **Lincoln Memorial**
Construction began: 1914
Construction finished: 1922
Made of: marble and limestone

2 **Washington Monument**
Construction began: 1848
Construction finished: 1888
Made of: marble and granite

3 **Jefferson Memorial**
Construction began: 1938
Construction finished: 1942
Made of: marble and limestone

4 **Vietnam Veterans Memorial**
Construction began: 1982
Construction finished: 1982
Made of: granite

Answer the questions. Use information from the map.

1. Which two memorials are closest to the Potomac? _____

_____

2. Which memorial is west of the Vietnam Veterans Memorial? _____

_____

3. Which of the four memorials took the longest to build? _____

_____

4. Why do you think that it took so long? What events at the time

   could have interfered? _____

_____

5. What materials were used to make these monuments? _____

_____

6. Why do you think these materials were used? _____

_____

Maya Lin said, "Some memorials are journeys or passages."[5]

How is this true about the Vietnam Veterans Memorial?

Connecting Today and Yesterday

1. What memorials have you visited? Which people or groups did they honor? What do you remember about their designs?

2. Do you think that cemeteries should also be used as parks? What do you think that the atmosphere of a cemetery should be?

Group Activity

Research the Vietnam Veterans Memorial in Washington, D.C., and the Civil Rights Memorial in Montgomery, Alabama. Bring information and photographs to class. Discuss these questions.

1. How are the two memorials the same? How are they different? What do you like about each memorial?

2. Do you think that the design of the Vietnam Veterans Memorial is patriotic? Explain.

Class Discussion

1. Why would Lin's parents not teach Lin or her brother the Chinese language or tell them about life in China? Would you have done the same? Why or why not?

2. In what ways do you think that her parents' careers influenced Lin's career choice?

3. Why did Lin face racism when her design became public?

4. Was Lin right not to change her original design for the Vietnam Veterans Memorial? Why or why not?

5. In recent years, Lin has worked on projects that express the need to protect the environment. Why does she feel that this is important? Do you agree with her? Why or why not?

Reflections

1. What was the most interesting thing that you read in this lesson?

2. Can you use anything from Maya Lin's story in your own life? Explain.

3. How can you learn more about Maya Lin or the Vietnam Veterans Memorial?

Notes and References

General References

Ambrose, Stephen E. *Undaunted Courage: Meriwether Lewis, Thomas Jefferson, and the Opening of the American West.* New York: Simon & Schuster, 1996.

McCullough, David. *John Adams.* New York: Simon & Schuster, 2001.

Miller Center of Public Affairs, University of Virginia. *AmericanPresident.org.* Online at www.americanpresident.org.

Morison, Samuel Eliot; Henry Steele Commager; and William E. Leuchtenburg. *A Concise History of the American Republic,* 2nd ed. New York: Oxford University Press, 1983.

Public Broadcasting Service. Web site of *American Experience,* www.pbs.org/wgbh/amex.

Rice, Arnold M.; John A. Krout; and Charles M. Harris. *United States History to 1877.* New York: Harper Perennial, 1991.

John Adams

Notes

1. David McCullough, *John Adams,* p. 15.
2. David McCullough, *John Adams,* p. 643.
3. David McCullough, *John Adams,* p. 127.
4. David McCullough, *John Adams,* p. 646.
5. Ralph Waldo Emerson, "Concord Hymn," 1837, in *Yale Book of American Verse,* Thomas R. Lounsbury, ed., New Haven: Yale University Press, 1912.
6. David McCullough, *John Adams,* p. 236.

References

Ellis, Joseph John. "Adams, John. " *Encyclopædia Britannica,* 2003. Text at *Encyclopædia Britannica Online,* www.search.eb.com/eb/article?eu=3706 (retrieved Oct. 6, 2003).

"John Adams." On the web site of the White House, www.whitehouse.gov/history/presidents/ja2.html (retrieved Aug, 11, 2002).

"Adams and Jefferson." 1997. On the web site of *Liberty! The American Revolution.* www.pbs.org/ktca/liberty/chronicle/adams-jefferson.html (retrieved Nov. 20, 2003).

Thomas Jefferson

Notes

1. Thomas Jefferson, *A Summary View of the Rights of British America,* 1774; reprinted in Thomas Jefferson, *Writings.*
2. David McCullough, *John Adams,* p. 114.
3. from a letter to Benjamin Rush, Sept. 23, 1800; quoted on the White House web site.
4. Thomas Jefferson, "First Inaugural Address," March 4, 1801; text on Bartleby.com.

References

Ellis, Joseph J. *American Sphinx: The Character of Thomas Jefferson.* New York: Alfred A. Knopf, 1997.

Ellis, Joseph. *Founding Brothers: The Revolutionary Generation.* Rockland, MA: Compass Press, 2000.

Jefferson, Thomas. *Writings,* Merrill D. Peterson, ed. New York: Library of America, Literary Classics of the United States, 1984.

Public Broadcasting Service. Web site for *Thomas Jefferson: A Film by Ken Burns,* 1996. Text at PBS Online, www.pbs.org/jefferson (retrieved July 4, 2002).

"Thomas Jefferson." On the web site of the White House. www.whitehouse.gov/history/presidents/tj32.html (retrieved Aug. 11, 2002).

"Thomas Jefferson. 1743–1826." John Bartlett, comp. 1919. *Familiar Quotations,* 10th ed. Text on Bartleby.com, www.bartleby.com/100/298.html (retrieved Nov. 21, 2003).

"Thomas Jefferson: The Revolution of 1800." *For Teachers: Inauguration 2001,* MacNeil/Lehrer Productions, 2001. *Online NewsHour,* www.pbs.org/newshour/inauguration/lesson_jefferson.html (retrieved Dec. 13, 2002).

Wingert, Pat. "Jefferson's Other Family." *Newsweek.* Feb. 7, 2000. p. 57.

"The Works of Thomas Jefferson." 1995. *Liberty Online,* libertyonline.hypermall.com/Jefferson/index.html (retrieved July 3, 2002).

Meriwether Lewis

Notes

1. William Clark," November 7, 1805," in *Journals of Lewis and Clark.*
2. Meriwether Lewis, "August 18, 1805," in *Journals of Lewis and Clark.*

References

Bredenberg, Al. *The Expedition of the Corps of Discovery: An Overview of the Lewis and Clark Expedition.* Smithsonian Institution and EdGate.com, Inc., 2000. Text at www.edgate.com/lewisandclark/expedition.html (retrieved Aug. 15, 2003).

Journals of Lewis and Clark, text on the web site of the American Studies program at the University of Virginia, xroads.virginia.edu/~HYPER/JOURNALS/journals.html (retrieved May 24, 2004).

"Meriwether Lewis." On the web site for *New Perspectives on the West,* 1996, www.pbs.org/weta/thewest/people/i_r/lewis.htm (retrieved Dec. 5, 2003).

National Park Service. *Lewis and Clark Expedition: A National Register of Historic Places Travel Itinerary.* National Park Service web site, www.cr.nps.gov/nr/travel/lewisandclark (retrieved Aug. 15, 2003).

National Park Service, *Lewis & Clark National Historic Trail,* National Park Service web site, www.nps.gov/lecl/ (retrieved June 27, 2002).

Public Broadcasting Service. Web site for *Lewis & Clark: The Journey of the Corps of Discovery: A Film by Ken Burns, 1997.* www.pbs.org/lewisandclark (retrieved March 28, 2002).

Frederick Douglass

Notes

1. Frederick Douglass, *Narrative of the Life of Frederick Douglass,* Chapter 10.

2. Frederick Douglass, "My Escape from Slavery."

3. John F. Kennedy, *Profiles in Courage,* New York: Harper, 1956, p. 246; quoted in *Respectfully Quoted: A Dictionary of Quotations Requested from the Congressional Research Service.* Washington D.C.: Library of Congress, 1989.

References

Douglass, Frederick. *Narrative of the Life of Frederick Douglass, An American Slave.* Boston: Anti-Slavery Office, 1845. Text at *University of California, Berkeley Digital Library Sun SITE,* sunsite.berkeley.edu/Literature/Douglass/Autobiography/10.html (retrieved May 24, 2004).

Douglass, Frederick. "My Escape from Slavery." *The Century Illustrated Magazine,* Nov. 1881, pp. 125–131. Text at *About African-American History,* afroamhistory.about.com/library/bldouglass_escape.htm (retrieved July 13, 2004).

"Douglass, Frederick," in *The Encyclopædia Britannica Guide to Black History,* Tom Michael, ed., 1997. Text at *Encyclopædia Britannica Online,* search.eb.com/blackhistory/micro/176/64.html (retrieved Dec. 14, 2003).

"Frederick Douglass," on the web site for *Africans in America,* 1998. www.pbs.org/wgbh/aia/part4/4p1539.html (retrieved Dec. 14, 2003).

Harriet Beecher Stowe

Notes

1. *Providence Mirror,* 1852; quoted in a Jewett & Co. advertisement, *The New York Independent,* May 20, 1852; text on the web site of The Institute for Advanced Technology in the Humanities, University of Virginia, www.iath.virginia.edu/utc/reviews/read12at.html (retrieved May 24, 2004).

2. "Harriet's Life and Times."

3. from a letter to Gamaliel Bailey, March 9, 1851; quoted in E. Bruce Kirkham, *Libraries, Mrs. Stowe, and Me,* Muncie, IN: Kirkham Lecture to the Friends of the Alexander M. Bracken Library, 2001; text on the web site of Ball State University, www.bsu.edu/library/media/pdf/kirkham_book.pdf (retrieved May 25, 2004).

4. Harriet Beecher Stowe, as quoted in Annie Fields, "Days with Mrs. Stowe," *The Atlantic Monthly,* Vol. 78, Issue 466, August 1896, p. 146.

References

"Harriet's Life and Times," 2001; on the web site of the Harriet Beecher Stowe Center, www.harrietbeecherstowe.org/life/ (retrieved Dec. 7, 2003).

Hedrick, Joan D. *Harriet Beecher Stowe: A Life.* New York: Little Brown and Co., 1994.

"Stowe, Harriet Beecher," in *Women in American History by Encyclopædia Britannica,* 1999. Text at *Encyclopædia Britannica Online,* women.eb.com/women/articles/Stowe_Harriet_Beecher.html (retrieved March 11, 2002).

Walt Whitman

Notes

1. Roy Morris Jr., *The Better Angel,* p. 143.

2. "America's Wars," Washington, D.C.: Department of Veterans Affairs, Office of Public Affairs, May 2001; on the web site of the Department of Veterans Affairs, http://www.va.gov/pressrel/amwars01.htm (retrieved July 9, 2004).

3. Walt Whitman, "The Wounded for Chancellorsville."

4. Walt Whitman, *Leaves of Grass,* preface to the first edition.

References

"A Poet of the People." On *Learning Adventures in Citizenship,* a companion web site to *New York: A Documentary Film,* www.pbs.org/wnet/newyork/laic/episode2/topic7/e2_t7_s1-pp.html (retrieved May 18, 2002).

Folsom, Ed, and Kenneth M. Price. "Walt Whitman." *The Walt Whitman Archive,* www.whitmanarchive.org/criticism/biography/biography.html (retrieved July 13, 2004).

Morris, Roy, Jr. *The Better Angel: Walt Whitman in the Civil War.* New York: Oxford University Press, 2000.

Morris, Roy, Jr. "Review of *Walt Whitman: The Song of Himself,* by Jerome Loving." *America's Civil War,* Jan. 2000, vol. 12, issue 6, p. 58.

"Walt Whitman." 2001. On the web site of The Academy of American Poets, www.poets.org/poets/poets.cfm?45442B7C000C07070E (retrieved Dec. 16, 2003).

Whitman, Walt. "The Wounded for Chancellorsville," in *Prose Works,* Philadelphia: David Mackay, 1892; text at www.bartleby.com/229/1033.html (retrieved June 17, 2004).

Whitman, Walt. *Leaves of Grass,* preface to the first edition; quoted in Anthony Szczesiul, "Walt Whitman and the Development of *Leaves of Grass,*" Columbia, SC: Thomas Cooper Library, University of South Carolina, 1992; text on the web site of the Libraries of the University of South Carolina, www.sc.edu/library/spcoll/amlit/whitman/ww1.html (retrieved May 25, 2004).

Elizabeth Cady Stanton

Notes

1. from a letter to Thomas Wentworth Higginson, 1868; quoted in James Ishmael Ford, "The Spiritual Citizen," 1999; text on the web site of Valley Unitarian Universalist Church, Chandler, Arizona, www.vuu.org/jford/ss991017.htm (retrieved May 25, 2004).

2. Elizabeth Cady Stanton, "A Declaration of Sentiments."

References

Public Broadcasting Service. Web site for *Not for Ourselves Alone: The Story of Elizabeth Cady Stanton and Susan B. Anthony,* www.pbs.org/stantonanthony/ (retrieved July 8, 2002).

Rynder, Constance, "All Men and Woman Are Created Equal," *American History,* August 1998, vol. 33, issue 3, pp. 22–28.

Stanton, Elizabeth Cady. "A Declaration of Sentiments," Seneca Falls Women's Rights Convention, 1848; text in *Basic Readings in U.S. Democracy,* on the web site of International Information Programs, U.S. Department of State, usinfo.state.gov/usa/infousa/facts/democrac/17.htm (retrieved May 25, 2004).

Ward, Geoffrey. *Not for Ourselves Alone.* New York: Alfred A. Knopf, 1999.

Eugene V. Debs

Notes

1. Eugene V. Debs, "The Issue," speech given on May 23, 1908; text on the web site of School of Communication, Northwestern University, douglassarchives.org/debs_a80. htm (retrieved May 25, 2004).

2. quoted on the web site of the Labor Hall of Fame, U.S. Department of Labor, www.dol.gov/oasam/programs/ laborhall/evd.htm (retrieved May 25, 2004).

References

"Eugene V. Debs." 2000. On the web site of the Indiana Historical Society, www.indianahistory.org/heritage/evdebs. html (retrieved Dec. 21, 2003).

Radosh, Ronald. *Debs: Great Lives Observed.* Prentice-Hall, 1971.

Web site of the Eugene V. Debs Foundation, www. eugenevdebs.com/index.htm, (retrieved July 11, 2002).

Zinn, Howard. "Eugene V. Debs and the Idea of Socialism." *The Progressive,* Jan. 1999, vol. 63, no. 1. pp. 16–18.

Dorothea Lange

Notes

1. a Kansas preacher, 1936; quoted on the web site of "Surviving the Dust Bowl," *American Experience,* Public Broadcasting Service, www.pbs.org/wgbh/amex/dustbowl/ peopleevents/pandeAMEX08.html (retrieved May 25, 2004).

2. quoted in *Los Angeles Times,* Aug. 13, 1978. Cited in *The Columbia World of Quotations,* New York: Columbia University Press, 1996.

3. Louis C. Gawthrop, "Dorothea Lange and Visionary Change."

References

Dorothea Lange, in The History of Photography Series. Millerton, NY: Aperture, Inc. 1981.

Gawthrop, Louis C. "Dorothea Lange and Visionary Change." *Society,* July/Aug. 1993, vol. 30, issue 5, p. 65.

Perchick, Max. "Dorothea Lange." *PSA Journal,* June 1995, vol 61, issue 6, p. 26.

Felix Frankfurter

Notes

1. Clare Cushman, ed. *The Supreme Court Justices: Illustrated Biographies,* 1789–1993. p. 390.

2. from Readers Digest, June 1964; quoted in *Simpson's Contemporary Quotations,* compiled by James B. Simpson, Boston: Houghton Mifflin, 1988.

3. John Bartlett, compiler. *Familiar Quotations,* 10th ed, rev. and enl. by Nathan Haskell Dole. Boston: Little, Brown, 1919; text at www.bartleby.com/100/(retrieved June 17, 2004).

References

Breyer, Stephen J. "Zion's Justice." *The New Republic,* Oct. 5, 1998, vol. 219, no. 14, pp. 18–19.

Cushman, Clare, ed. *The Supreme Court Justices: Illustrated Biographies,* 1789–1993. Washington, D.C.: Congressional Quarterly, Inc., 1993.

"Felix Frankfurter," *The Columbia Encyclopedia,* 6th ed., New York: Columbia University Press, 2001.

Goldman, Jerry. "Felix Frankfurter: Biography." On the web site *OYEZ: U.S. Supreme Court Multimedia.* www.oyez.org/ oyez/resource/legal_entity/78/biography (retrieved Dec. 7, 2003).

Rachel Carson

Notes

1. "The Silent Spring of Rachel Carson," *CBS Reports,* broadcast April 3, 1963; quoted in "Rachel Carson Dies of Cancer; 'Silent Spring' Author Was 56," *New York Times,* April 15, 1964.

2. E. Cheraskin, "Detoxification: A Must for the New Millennium," *Journal of Orthomolecular Medicine,* Second Quarter 2000, vol. 15, no. 2.

3. an unnamed expert on natural resources, quoted in Frank Graham, Jr. "Rachel Carson."

References

"Biography: Rachel Louise Carson." On the web site of RachelCarson.org, www.rachelcarson.org/index. cfm?fuseaction=bio (retrieved Dec. 26, 2003).

Carson, Rachel. *Silent Spring.* Boston: Houghton Mifflin, 1962.

Graham, Frank, Jr. "Rachel Carson." *EPA Journal,* Nov./Dec. 1978. Text online at www.epa.gov/history/topics/perspect/ carson.htm (retrieved Dec 26, 2003).

Matthiessen, Peter. "Rachel Carson," in *The Time 100: The Most Important People of the Century,* 1999. Text online at www. time.com/time/time100/scientist/profile/ carson.html (retrieved Dec. 26, 2003).

"People and Discoveries: Rachel Carson," 1998. On the web site of *A Science Odyssey,* www.pbs.org/wgbh/aso/databank/ entries/btcars.html (retrieved Dec. 26, 2003).

"The Power of One," in *People & Profiles.* 2000. On the web site of the U.S. Environmental Protection Agency, www.epa. gov/epahome/people2_0608.htm (retrieved Dec. 26, 2003).

César Chávez

Notes

1. "The Story of César Chávez."

2. "The Story of César Chávez."

References

Levy, Jacques. *Cesar Chavez: Autobiography of La Causa.* New York: W.W. Norton & Co., 1975.

Matthiessan, Peter, *Sal Si Puedes; Cesar Chavez and the New American Revolution.* New York: Random House, 1969.

Public Broadcasting Service. Web site for *The Fight in the Fields: Cesar Chavez and the Farmworkers' Struggle,* 1997. Text at PBS Online, www.pbs.org/itvs/fightfields (retrieved July 21, 2004).

United Farm Workers. *UFW: Official web site of the United Farm Workers,* www.ufw.org (retrieved May 25, 2004).

Rosa Parks

Notes

1. "Dec. 1, 1955: A Bus Rider's Defiance"

2. quoted in "Rosa Parks, Pioneer of Civil Rights, Biography."

3. quoted in "Rosa Parks: Pioneer for Civil Rights."

References

Albin, Kira. "Rosa Parks: The Woman Who Changed a Nation," 1996. On the web site *GRANDtimes.com,* http://www.grandtimes.com/rosa.html (retrieved July 21, 2004).

"Dec. 1, 1955: A Bus Rider's Defiance," *80 Days That Changed the World;* text on the web site of *Time Online Edition,* www.time.com/time/80days/551201.html (retrieved May 25, 2004).

Moritz, Charles, editor. "Parks, Rosa," *Current Biography Yearbook,* 1989. New York: H.W. Wilson, pp. 431–434.

Parks, Rosa, with Jim Haskins. *Rosa Parks: My Story.* New York: Dial Books, 1992.

Rosa and Raymond Parks Institute for Self Development. *Official web site of the Rosa and Raymond Parks Institute,* www.rosaparksinstitute.org (retrieved July 21, 2004).

"Rosa Parks: Pioneer for Civil Rights," *Portraits of Character from the National Portrait Gallery,* on the web site of the Smithsonian Institution, www.npg.si.edu/inf/edu/rosa.htm (retrieved May 25, 2004).

"Rosa Parks, Pioneer of Civil Rights, Biography." 2003. On the web site of the Academy of Achievement, www.achievement.org/autodoc/page/par0bio-1 (retrieved July 15, 2004).

Billy Frank, Jr.

Notes

1. Billy Frank, Jr., "Everyone Should Celebrate the Makah Whale Hunt," June 2, 1999, text in the PEN-L mailing list archive, archives.econ.utah.edu/archives/pen-l/1999m06.b/msg00166.htm (retrieved May 25, 2004).

2. Beth Hege Piatote, "Against the Current," p. 104.

3. Carol Jacobs, "Presentation to the United Nations, July 18, 1995"; published in *Akwesasne Notes,* Fall 1995, Vol. 1, No. 3 & 4, pp. 116-117; text at www.ratical.org/many_worlds/6Nations/ PresentToUN.html (retrieved June 17, 2004).

References

Biography Resource Center. "Billy Frank Jr." Gale Group, Inc. 2001. Text on the web site *Native North Americans,* www.nativepubs.com/nativepubs/Apps/bios/0162FrankBilly.asp (retrieved Dec. 16, 2003).

Piatote, Beth Hege. "Against the Current," in *A Place at the Table: Struggles for Equality in America,* ed. Maria Fleming, New York: Oxford University Press, 2003, pp. 98–107.

Maya Lin

Notes

1. "Re: Vietnam: Stories Since the War."

2. Louis Menand, "The Reluctant Memorialist."

3. "I Have a Dream," speech given August 28, 1963, text in *Basic Readings in U.S. Democracy,* on the web site of the International Information Programs, U.S. Department of State, usinfo.state.gov/usa/infousa/facts/democrac/38.htm (retrieved May 25, 2004).

4. "Maya Lin Interview."

5. "The Art of Honoring the Dead."

References

"Architect Maya Lin" on the web site *Great Buildings Online,* www.greatbuldings.com/architects/Maya_Lin.html (retrieved Nov. 30, 2003).

"The Art of Honoring the Dead," signed "C.M.," *Newsweek,* Sept. 9, 2002.

"Maya Lin Interview," June 16, 2000; text on the web site of the Academy of Achievement, www.achievement.org/autodoc/page/lin0int-8 (retrieved June 21, 2004).

Menand, Louis. "The Reluctant Memorialist." *The New Yorker,* July 8, 2002.

"Re: Vietnam: Stories Since the War" on the Public Broadcasting Service web site, www.pbs.org/pov/stories/vietnam/story.html (retrieved May 25, 2004).